Bron Lewis left her decade-long career as a high school teacher to become an award-winning stand-up comedian. She is now a regular panellist on Channel Ten's *Have You Been Paying Attention?*, a co-host of three podcasts, *Good Sheilas*, *Work Hates* and *Your Two Drunk Aunties*, and a core cast member of the ABC sketch show, *Urzila*.

A mother to three young children, her 2024 show 'Obviously' not only sold out all around the country but poignantly tackled the subject area of women's mental health in general, specifically postnatal anxiety and depression. Her consecutive stand-up shows also sold out nationwide, and always give a nod to the gendered experience. Hilarious, ridiculous and honest, Bron Lewis is a star on the rise.

I'M NOT MAD
(ANYMORE)

BRON LEWIS

affirm press

affirm press

First published in Australia in 2026 by Affirm Press,
a Simon & Schuster (Australia) Pty Limited company
Wurundjeri Woiwurrung Country
Level 3, 162 Collins Street, Melbourne VIC 3000
Affirm Press is located on the unceded land of the Wurundjeri Woiwurrung peoples of the Kulin Nation. Affirm Press pays respect to their Elders past and present.

New York Amsterdam/Antwerp London Toronto Sydney/Melbourne New Delhi
Visit our website at www.simonandschuster.com.au

10 9 8 7 6 5 4 3 2 1

NATIONAL LIBRARY OF AUSTRALIA
A catalogue record for this book is available from the National Library of Australia

9781923135918 (paperback)
9781761822445 (ebook)

Cover design by Luke Causby/Blue Cork
Cover image by Chris Hillary
Typeset by J&M Typesetting in 12/19.5 pt Garamond Premier Pro
Printed and bound in Australia by the Opus Group

FSC www.fsc.org
MIX
Paper from responsible sources
FSC® C001695

For my kids, Olive, Edith and Ari you will always be the best thing I've ever made.

CONTENTS

PROLOGUE

Hi, I'm Bron Lewis. Some of you may know me from stand-up comedy, or various telly shows, or from when I was a run-of-the-mill high school teacher, burnt out and under-appreciated. But the lucky ones will know me from when I lost my mind.

If you have come here for my comedy, congratulations, there are many funny bits if I do say so myself. I would be lying if I said every chapter was funny, though. I have tried to sugarcoat some of the most painfully horrible moments of my life, but sometimes there just isn't enough sugar in the world.

This book that you find yourself reading is the book I wanted to read when I was mad. My first baby, Olive, screamed bloody murder for the first six months of her life and, to drown out the screaming, I would walk the freezing streets of Brunswick, Melbourne. Olive was rugged up within an inch of her life while I listened to Clare Bowditch's song 'You Make Me Happy' on repeat, hoping it would rub off on me and my miserable baby girl.

One particularly frigid day I saw an Italian nonna storming towards me, no doubt armed with a lecture about having a baby outside in winter, which is, from what I can gather after all my years in Brunswick, a nonna's favourite thing to berate a tired new mum about. Fearful that I was at the end of my tether and I would meet her scolding with a tirade of my own, I escaped into a quaint little bookshop. I filled its peaceful silence with Olive's unbridled wailing and my incessant apologies about having the world's most unhappy baby.

I caught my reflection in the mirror behind a pile of bright books with thunderous fonts and didn't recognise myself. My skin was grey, my chapped lips were thinner than ever and the bags under my eyes were sinking towards my chin. I hadn't dyed my hair in a couple of months, so the mousy brown regrowth was now a prominent strip down the centre of my scalp, and the red hair was dull and drab, like a scrappy garage-sale poster left in the elements. I reminded myself of the kind of lady I would have avoided eye contact with in case our fleeting human connection made her grab my hands and ugly-cry about how she was once the prettiest girl in Year 10 and now she was completely invisible. Maybe I was that woman. I mean, I wasn't the prettiest girl in Year 10 – not a single boy had offered to pash me – but, aside from being accosted by Brunswick nonnas, I may as well have been invisible.

'Why am I so shit at this?' I thought. 'What have I got so wrong?'

Fighting back tears, I searched for a book that had some answers, something I found myself doing countless times in moments of desperation. Unfortunately, books on parenting are almost always written by self-righteous twats who are either too militant or too whimsical for my taste. I picked them up, read their blurbs and put them back, like a shoe that didn't fit. Olive's crying ramped up, so I quickly grabbed a book, paid for it and squeezed my eyes shut, hoping that it would, please, for the love of Christmas, solve everything.

I did read that book and, SURPRISE, it did not save me. It was about a single mother who was struggling so badly that she left her baby in the apartment all day to scream while she tried to piece together the life she'd had before she became a mother. I hated that book. It was visceral and unrelatable: I wouldn't have been able to leave my baby in an apartment by herself when I found it nearly impossible to go to a different *room*.

I have had three beautiful children and, not coincidentally, I have gone mad three times – all different flavours of mad. Each time I searched for a book that I could relate to, and each time I failed to find it. We tell women that motherhood is glorious, and yet we all know deep down that there are days, weeks, months, sometimes years when you're in a living hell, and not necessarily because of your children (well, sometimes), but because of your hormonal brain, which tells you you're fucking everything up (and, yes, sometimes you are – whoopsie-daisy).

It is wild to me that such a universal experience of motherhood can be muzzled the way it is. We consume sugar-coated versions of it from movies, literature and mummy influencers, so when we do venture into motherhood ourselves, the cold snap of reality feels like an unforgivable betrayal of all those who neglected to warn us. If we admit we find motherhood hard, we risk being the only voice out there doing so, so we say nothing but words of gratitude. 'I'm the luckiest woman alive,' 'I can't believe I waited so long to have her' and 'I wouldn't see any point in my life without him.' Do we mean that? Yeah, annoyingly we do, but these, like all thoughts, are fleeting, just like the negative ones. We are banned from saying, 'I miss my old life,' 'I wish I waited a while longer before I had them' or 'This is genuinely the most fucked thing I've ever done' because if these thoughts are uttered aloud, we risk being shunned entirely. Motherhood is supposed to be smothered in gratitude, so we grit our teeth, smile, rock our screaming babies and wait for the part when it gets easier.

It took me years to write this book. I'm referring not just to the physical side – bashing my fingers on a keyboard for countless hours and yelling down the hallway, 'ASK YOUR FATHER, MUMMY'S WRITING A BOOK!' – but also to the mental side. That took a while. I knew that if I needed a book about going mad, other women probably wanted one, too, but for a long time I was too overwhelmed to even brush my hair, let alone write a book. Plus, I was far too close to the flames of hell to find the words to describe it, so, like sleep, this book needed to wait until I had enough space and forgiveness to pull it off. I'm not entirely sure I've reached a healthy dose of either of these things, but I don't know if anyone ever does. So here is the book I needed to read when I felt like I was failing at the most important job I would ever have. The book I longed for when I felt like I was completely alone. The book I needed when I was mad.

The longer I live, the more convinced I am that we expect women to go mad. I bet you couldn't find an honest person who didn't say their mother was a bit loopy, and frankly it makes sense that us women do lose our footing at some point in our lives. Under the weight of the ever-growing mental load, the constant and sometimes violent hormonal shifts, the expectation of looking a certain way, fostering a career to prove to everyone that women are capable of doing it all while keeping everyone in the family alive, it would make sense the old mental health would fray. We cope with watching our mothers lose their minds by creating a common ground where we can laugh at our collective experience. If we laugh together, it's an acceptable joke, right?

Most of us have memories of our bewildered mothers being dragged through menopause, kicking and screaming like a toddler being forcibly removed from the zoo gift shop.

I am brutally honest about my mother in this book. Don't worry yourselves sick about it: Helen has read the chapters about her and given me her blessing. The night before I submitted the manuscript to the publisher, we sat in my backyard with a bottle of white wine and I gave her one last chance to change her mind. She smiled and said, 'It's all true, so I'm happy for you to publish it. I'm sorry you had to live through that, darling.' She took a long drag from her cigarette. 'But could you please take out any reference to me being a smoker? Some people think I've quit.' I lied and said I would. (As if anyone on the face of this planet thinks Hels will ever give up her beloved ciggies.) It wasn't easy to write about Mum's mental break. Her battle with menopause almost broke her, and it changed not only how we saw her, but how she saw herself.

We expect women to go mad, but we don't give them the tools to manage it. We think we're getting better at it, but I don't think we are even close to where we should be. In the 16th century, women who acted out of character were accused of being witches and burnt at the stake. (They were usually women who had recently become mothers or women who were experiencing 'the change' – coincidence?) It doesn't surprise me at all that the highest suicide rate for females is in the age range of 45–49, and the second highest is 50–54, meaning the menopausal years for a lot of women are, statistically speaking, unliveable. We may not be burning women alive anymore, but we are burying them under a pile of their own raging hormones and undeserving shame.

To be a woman is to have secrets, and I, like everyone, come from a long line of secretive women. My mother, grandmothers and great-grandmothers probably had a million secrets stuffed deep inside them, weighed down by instant mashed potato (yum) and guilt (ew). From a young age we learn that when we become mothers ourselves we will disappoint our children somehow, and only some of us will be lucky enough to redeem ourselves. It's in our nature to show our best face, even when we are completely bonkers, screaming into the void with our tits swinging in the wind. You know, normal stuff.

Most people die with their secrets, but I will not. I will die with a belly full of instant mashed potato and the knowledge that I have upset the apple cart unapologetically. I'll die knowing that I tried my very best as a mother to three beautiful children and, despite this, failed them and myself countless times. I'll die having forgiven my mother and hoping that she forgave herself along the way. I'll die having forgiven myself. I am not there yet, but hopefully I won't die any time soon.

My wish is that this book might shine a tiny light on the darkest parts of being a woman and perhaps allow us to laugh at those parts, or just acknowledge that they exist. Whether it makes you hold a mirror up to yourself or allows you to see your mother, sister or daughter differently, I hope you do so with kindness. I hope my humiliating anecdotes, small wins and catastrophic near misses bring you light in a dark moment. But mostly I hope this book brings you some solace from some of the cruellest memories your brain has latched on to. We all deserve at least that.

MUM'S PARENTING STYLE

I always knew my mum was a bit different to most mums. She had five kids (four of whom were solely her responsibility), a business she ran from our dining-room table and a tendency to go mad. It makes sense to me that she would sometimes go mad – who wouldn't with that much on their plate? Most of us would drop the ball with only one of those ~~burdens mistakes hobbies~~ responsibilities.

With five kids, it's no surprise that she wasn't a helicopter mum. She was more of a hot air balloon mum – she'd just float about aimlessly hoping for the best, sometimes bursting into flames.

I know now, having three kids, that your 'trust' in them to do things for themselves kicks in younger the more kids you have. I was like a pit bull with my first, a labrador with my second and a 'missing dog' sign with my third. Kids are resilient, and parenting is exhausting, so this trust is a survival technique. If you are the third-born, or, god help you, the fourth or fifth, chances are your parents raised you with a combination of devon, telly and hope.

If you are the third-, fourth- or fifth-born, don't resent your parents – look at you now! You can read! (Unless, of course, you're listening to this on an audiobook and, if so, well done on getting this far in life. Avoiding literacy is a skill far more impressive than reading.) If you are, in fact, reading this, it certainly wasn't your parents who taught you – you just survived long enough to teach yourself, so this parenting technique works. Be #grateful that you are #literate or #pretendingtobeliterate.

As the third-born, I could get away with a lot of things. It was a crying shame that I wasn't a particularly rebellious kid: the lack of supervision was wasted on me. I did get away with Mum never reading my report card, because she had given up on caring about them. I was a pretty good kid and, as far as she could tell, I could read (again, not her handiwork), so I was fine.

I was a dreadful student, though, so it wouldn't have hurt for her to read the report cards. I rarely handed anything in, and if I did it was very late. For almost every assignment, I wrote a note that said *Bron needs an extension on this project as we have had a family emergency*, and I would sign it with a signature that kind of looked like my stepdad's. I made it up in Year 7, and continued this identity theft until the end of Year 12. It was like I knew in Year 7 that I was going to be the worst student ever, which was probably the only thing I got right at school.

I also skipped class more often than I attended. On the last day of Year 10, awards were handed out – 'Best athlete', 'Best musician', 'Most likely to be Prime Minister', et cetera – and I was given an award I worked really hard on: 'Wagged the most classes'. My terrible attendance and dreadful output would have been in my school reports, but we'll never know for sure. On the day they were handed out, I would exit the classroom and unashamedly throw my report in the bin. Kids would gasp, but I just assured them that my mum wasn't like their mums, because she wasn't.

She was eclectic and busy and distracted and on a slippery slope to madness. My report card was the least of her worries.

Mum's trust that I would do the right thing and keep myself safe was pushed to the limits a few times. When I was fifteen, she let me travel to China to visit my big brother, Hamish, who had moved there to teach English when he was seventeen. So I guess she used the 'third-child approach' for all her kids. By this stage, Hamish was eighteen and we travelled through China with almost no money. We had many close calls on this trip, and many moments that were well outside what was appropriate for our age bracket. One night we stayed in what we thought was a really cheap hotel, but was actually a very seedy brothel. When we realised what the place was, we locked ourselves in our revolting room and ate Pringles for dinner.

Mum laughed her head off when we told her about this, and when she laughed, so did we. Her blasé attitude was contagious, and when she chose the funny side of things, we followed. She was our hot air balloon after all.

It was my first trip overseas, and I figured all travelling experiences were riddled with extreme risk. Still, when I finished school (thank fucking Christ), I increased the hours at my three shitty hospitality jobs to save enough money to travel the world. Mum didn't ask where I was planning on going, she just knew that I was going, and that was enough information for her. I decided to get an around-the-world ticket, and if you've gathered anything about my application to study, you'll know that purchasing this ticket was all the preparation I needed.

The year I decided to travel was 2005 – the year of the idiots. In Australia, we had the Cronulla riots, the Bali Nine and Schapelle Corby. Idiots. It was a great year for me, though. I had recently turned eighteen and, like every single eighteen-year-old, I was given a gift on my birthday: the ability to know everything. And, boy oh boy, did I know *everything*. I mean, I was allowed to drive, drink, smoke, vote, have a credit card with a $5000 limit and go to internet cafes unsupervised. Not only was I all-knowing, but I was also instantly worldly. I may have spent my whole life in suburban Canberra, with school holidays at my nan's house on the outskirts of Wagga Wagga, but I studied International Literature for a term in Year 11 so, yeah, I was worldly. I didn't hand in any assignments, but I had read Kafka's *The Metamorphosis* and understood some of it. I knew everything.

A guy I went to high school with, who was also recently eighteen and all-knowing, suggested we use this newly acquired intelligence to travel to Senegal in West Africa. I mean, Africa seemed cool, and we'd both watched *Madagascar*, so we were sold. By the way, this guy doesn't come off very well in this story, so let's call him Lenny, because as much as I want to write his actual name, he's the kind of weasel who would sue me for defamation even though I should be suing him for ever talking to me.

Mum found out I was going to Africa, and she uncharacteristically stopped in her tracks. She told me to look up the crime rates in Senegal and, as with most homework, I pretended I did it. She had heard from one of her friends that Senegal was actually really dangerous for tourists, especially young white women, but I'd stayed in a Chinese brothel when I was fifteen and nothing bad happened, so I ignored her. She tried to put her foot down but, after eighteen years of never putting her foot down with me, there was nowhere for her foot to land. I was going to Senegal whether she liked it or not.

Lenny and I were just as confident in our new-found adulthood, which would have been unbearable for actual adults to witness. Sure, I still hadn't figured out how to pluck my eyebrows the same size and, sure, Lenny still had acne on his back so severe that it bled through his shirt, BUT WE WERE OFFICIALLY ADULTS, DAMMIT!

On the plane to Senegal, Lenny explained that it would be safer and easier for us to pretend we were married – people would take us more seriously and, as eighteen-year-olds, that was all we wanted. So, just like that, 10,000 metres above the planet, I was pretend-married to a boy pretending to be a man who had chronic backne. Cool.

Walking around the chaotic streets of Dakar, we both hid how overwhelmed we were. Three grown men with Snoop Dogg shirts and thick golden necklaces started following us, so we spoke loudly of our wedding in Canberra as if that would make them disappear. It didn't. They approached us, and explained that we could relax because they were 'artists'. Lenny was immediately relieved, which irked me to no end. His mum had a small collection of art in her hallway, so naturally Lenny knew everything about art – in fact, because of this, he was sure *he* was an artist.

The golden-chained men asked us to go see their art. I said, 'No thanks!' and Lenny said, 'My wife means yes please!' And I didn't mean yes please, not even a little bit. Lenny said that he was going with or without me, so, as I looked around the busy street full of strangers, I begrudgingly agreed to go with.

All I could see was my mum's face asking me to be careful, words I wasn't used to her saying, so I didn't know how to action. There were nine of us piled into a tiny hatchback that drove two hours to a tiny dusty village on the coast with no electricity or running water. I was terrified, and Lenny was insufferable. He kept wrapping his sweaty arm around my shoulder and talking loudly and confidently about his art collection.

The men would nod and smile at each other, which was not a good sign.

We waited all afternoon for them to show us the art they promised to show us, but they would just smile and take us to a new part of their village for people to gawk at us. We were like prize pigs, or worse: a punchline to a sinister joke we didn't understand yet. The day turned to night and the art was still nowhere to be seen, so when they suggested a walk on the beach under the stars, we said yes because it wasn't really a question – we were 100 per cent their hostages at this point. I knew it, but Lenny still acted like everything was really normal, which irked me to no end. We obediently followed them to the beach and hoped with all our might that there would be a tiny gallery on the shore where we would laugh and then return safely to our hotel. It will surprise no one to learn that there was no gallery, just a big, dark, empty beach and the cold realisation we were never going to see any art, maybe ever again. Lenny refused to look at me because deep down he knew this wasn't right. He cheerfully tried to keep the conversations with the men alive, but they had become quite silent all of a sudden. One of the blokes lit up a joint and puffed on it furiously. This wasn't unusual – he had been smoking them all day – but what was unusual was how everyone stopped to silently watch him, as if waiting for something to happen.

Out of the darkness a man emerged in an ill-fitting police uniform, thongs and a plastic badge. He stormed towards us, yelling, 'No drugs!' He tackled the man who was smoking the joint, and proceeded to kick him over and over and over in the head. It was the most violence I had ever seen in real life, and I was scared shitless. All of the other men screamed and wailed, and Lenny, for the first time in his entire life, was speechless.

Through a blood-soaked mouth, the man on the ground said to me, 'Unless you want to go to jail for the rest of your life, you have to give him five thousand dollars.'

Jail? I mean, this was 2005, the year of the idiots. I suddenly realised: I was the next Schapelle Corby. I imagined my mum crying, and the rest of Australia shaking their heads at the dumb girl from Canberra who thought she was capable of travelling to Africa. This was not going to happen. I needed my hot air balloon more than ever.

Realising I had to pretend I was the adult I needed to be, I got up and went to the ATM with two sniffling men and withdrew all the money the bank had lent me. I thought about whether I would tell Mum about this, or just throw the memory in the bin along with my report cards.

I'd left Lenny behind with the wailing man and policeman, and wondered if it was safe being without him. But then I realised nothing he'd done had made me safe, so the bigger question was whether that fucking idiot was safe without me. When we got back to the beach, Lenny was no longer with the others, and my whole body froze. 'Shit,' I thought, 'they've killed him.' And as I looked to the golden-chained men for an explanation, one of them said in broken English, 'Your husband is over there.'

Fortunately, Lenny wasn't dead, but unfortunately he was still Lenny. Instead of checking if I was okay, he was just sulking in the sand – you know, like an adult would.

We left Senegal knowing full well that we'd been swindled by those guys, but Lenny never admitted it. I lost $5000 of the bank's money, and Lenny lost his pretend wife. On the bright side I didn't become the next Schapelle Corby and, more importantly, I learnt to never again trust an eighteen-year-old boy with my life.

I can't say for sure I knew something bad was going to happen on that trip. I think I left to show everyone how brave and independent I was, but I was leaving my childhood home where Mum's menopausal storm was in full force, and nothing felt scarier than to be trapped there. Watching someone you need unravel in front of you is unbelievably confronting. I like to think I travelled to an incredibly dangerous corner of the world because I had something to prove, but really I just needed to get as far away from her as possible.

Do I regret going? Of course I do. I'm not one of those people who says 'I have no regrets, just life experiences.' I have heaps of regrets. One of them is going to Africa with dumb-fuck Lenny, and another is punishing my mother for her mental breakdown, even though, at the time, I didn't know that's what I was doing. Perhaps I went there to remind her that I needed her still, even though I felt like she'd been gone for years. She may have always been a 'hands-off' kind of mum, but ever since her brain starting losing the battle with her hormones, she'd evolved into a giant cockroach and I was the apple lodged in her back (I told you I'd read Kafka). I can't speak for my siblings, but when Mum hit menopause, she became unrecognisable to me and we became her burdens. I guess it's hard to value your own life when the person who gave it to you makes you feel like an inconvenience.

I know that will hurt her heart to read that, but her heart has hurt for a long time and none of this is news to her. I've never thought that I was the biggest victim of mum's unravelling; nor were my siblings. The person she hurt the most was herself, and she continues to punish herself for something she couldn't control.

We can punish our mums for a long time, whether consciously or not. I used to be cross with my mum for a lot of things, even (if you can believe it) for not knowing I got report cards. It may have seemed like an act of rebellion at the time, but in hindsight, I think I just wanted to show my friends how little my mum noticed me. I was publicly shaming her for being too busy for me when she could barely keep her head above the rising tide of her shitty mental health. We both let each other down, and I know we both feel regret like bruises that won't heal.

Some would consider Mum's parenting style to be unsafe and irresponsible. Hell, I'd raise an eyebrow if I saw another mum like her and I would definitely scold a mate if she let her eighteen-year-old daughter go to Africa with her shit-stain friend, but at the end of the day I am who I am because of her parenting. I don't know if Mum's parenting was the 'right' parenting, but it's the only parenting I was offered, and I'm grateful for it. I am still alive, I know how to read and, because she gave me the freedom to travel with Lenny, I now know a dickhead when I meet one. I can't get cross with her because I'm alive with the best life I could have imagined. So unless you want a hot air balloon ride, jog on.

BLACK AND WHITE TILES

Mum met Jurek when we four kids were aged five to eleven. It blew everyone's minds that a man with only one kid would want to get involved with a woman with four small kids. He was a Polish carpenter with blue eyes, a cheeky grin and a rusty vintage station wagon with bullet-hole stickers on the back of it. We thought he was the duck's nuts because he really loved us kids but, more importantly, he made Mum laugh like crazy. It wasn't long before he had moved in with us and we met his perfect twelve-year old daughter from his first marriage. Huge news for Spence Primary – the Lewis kids had a stepsister living in Lismore and, no, we did not know where Lismore was.

At this stage, we were living in a tiny government house in Spence, where seven human beings were jammed into a very modest three-bedroom home – the same home mum ran her business from, and where my older sister Amy punched me in the face and called me a 'lesbian pervert' for walking into our *shared* bedroom when she was changing into her pyjamas. She was so mean when we were young. Now she is the most glorious, loyal woman and spectacular mother you could find; still, she punched me square in the nose when I was ten, and that deserves to be acknowledged for the rest of time. Could that be the reason I wrote this book? Probably. Justice comes in all shapes and sizes, bitch.

Mum thought Jurek would run for the hills the first time he saw our miniature house, but he didn't. It was very obviously commission housing; while each city in Australia has a slightly different style for its commission houses, the Canberran ones built in the 1970s had to be the ugliest (no offence if you live in one, I'm sure yours is the exception). These houses were a far cry from those designed by esteemed architects, and whoever did the heating in them was a dumb dog. It was so freezing that we could see our breath inside during winter, and after our baths we would sprint naked to the solitary electric heater in the lounge room and get so close we'd burn our bare bums on it. These freezing houses had either grey or light sandy-coloured bricks and the roof tiles only just reached the top of the bricks, so they looked like a kid who had accidentally given himself a zero-guard buzz cut. The windows looked like an oversight, as if they'd built the house without them, then, deciding even poor people needed light, knocked down some of the bricks and shoved in a mission-brown aluminium-framed window, which shook noisily in the wind. Mum tried her best to keep the house clean, but it was like pushing shit uphill: the tiles in the kitchen were brown and always looked dirty, even when they weren't. Mum hated those kitchen tiles.

In primary school I used to be proud of our tiny Spence house because it was one of the nicest houses on the street, and all my friends lived in similar ones. Mum had painted the front door a deep maroon and you could tell that whoever lived there was really proud of it. I knew it wasn't a mansion – I wasn't a bloody idiot – but compared to most of the other houses on our street, which had collections of broken cars on the front lawn and ripped curtains in the windows, it was pretty glorious.

I would walk up the driveway each afternoon with my tartan backpack and Ren and Stimpy hat and admire the garden Mum had worked so hard on. She'd almost broken her back making that garden beautiful, with roses and a pergola, where she'd sit and smoke. The bathroom window backed onto the pergola, and when my brother Simon was four and I was six, we overheard Mum sitting at the back table talking while we were in the bath. Curious, we climbed our slippery little bodies up onto the bathroom vanity, carefully slid open the rusty window and looked down at her to see who she was talking to. There she was, in her nursing home uniform with the top buttons undone and a tortoiseshell clip shoved into her short hair, talking to ... no one. Uh-oh. Mum, our only present parent, had lost it. We checked and checked again, but there was definitely no one there for her to talk to, so eventually we called out to her. 'Mum? Who are you talking to?' She looked up at us and burst out laughing, covering her face with her hands and howling. Doubled over, with tears streaming down her face, she laughed and laughed and laughed and Simon and I slowly slid the window shut and climbed back into the warm bath, feeling uneasy with confusion, but also relief to see her that free with joy.

It wasn't until years later that she told us she wasn't speaking to herself. She was actually practising for a university presentation that she was really nervous about. I treasure that memory: my beautiful mother falling to bits with laughter as Simon and I huddled in a window above her. Sure, she was single-handedly juggling four kids, a full-time job and a uni degree, but these were simpler times for us as a family. Just us four kids and our incredible mum. We had the least money at that point, but I dare say it was the happiest we ever were together.

Jurek moved into our humble Spence 'govvy', and within three years, our little sister Rosie was born: the greatest gift our family has ever received. We were all besotted with this perfect blonde baby girl, but none of us more so than Jurek. He would strap her to his back and go for long bushwalks to look for fairies. When they returned, the baby carrier was decorated with so much bright yellow wattle that Rosie looked ready for an Anne Geddes shoot.

It wasn't until Mum sent me to a posh high school that I became ashamed of our little house. The concept of class spilled into my life and it was confronting to realise I was dangling down the bottom end of it. I came to understand I had the shittest house out of all my friends by a country mile. One of my friends had a tennis court and a fridge with two vertical doors on it like you see in the movies. I liked going to other people's houses because if I was there, they couldn't see just how different my house was; all I needed to do was pretend their house wasn't blowing my tiny mind. Once, Jurek picked me up from the tennis-court house and mistakenly parked our Tarago on the strip of lush grass next to their driveway. The dad pulled up behind Jurek in his fancy BMW and held the horn down until he moved the car. I know now that this was the act of a fucking arsehole, but at the time, as a thirteen-year-old desperate to fit into a different class – or at the very least be secretly poor – I was just so embarrassed. I sat in the very back row of the Tarago on the way home and let my body fill with resentment towards Jurek, the man who intentionally humiliated me by damaging my rich friend's grass – also known as the bloke who was kind enough to pick me up and accidentally park on sacred grass, resulting in him being abused by some flog who thought he were better than him. Poor bastard.

I was fourteen when we moved to the big house in Queanbeyan, just outside of Canberra. Jurek built it himself – it took him about a decade to complete. For years we pored over the blueprints, dreaming about the day we'd get to move in, and when we did I was beside myself. Finally we lived like all the rich kids. We had a double-storey house with two lounge rooms and two bathrooms! The kitchen was by far the best bit, though – it was rustic, with black and white tiles that looked like they were out of a *Better Homes and Gardens* magazine. Mum was most proud of those tiles, and she joked that if she didn't get them, she wouldn't move in. She was right: they did look spectacular against the rich wooden cabinetry and fancy new fridge (embarrassingly with only one door). I can only speculate, but I think Mum thought those black and white tiles would erase all of the mistakes she had made and might prove to everyone she was actually a huge success. She didn't know it at the time, but there isn't a tile in the world that can withstand that much weight.

Goodbye, Porpoise Spence! I had made it! I wouldn't be the girl at school with the shittest house anymore, and I was over the fucking moon about it. I mean, it was a shame we had to move to Queanbe-hole for me to shake that title, but nothing in life is perfect. Shout out to Queanbeyan: may it burn to the ground.

Hamish, my oldest brother, only lived with us for a month or two after we moved in, which was devastating for me because he was my closest ally. He was seventeen, and originally I thought he was mental for wanting to bail on this class upgrade for a shitty share house in Canberra. It wasn't long before I understood the vibe in our new house was completely miserable, which took us all by surprise. So almost as soon as we had moved in, it was just Amy, sixteen, me, fourteen, Simon, twelve, Rosie, four, Jurek, forty-seven, and Mum, forty-five. The ages seem silly to list, but it's important for you to see that there were two teenage girls, an almost teenage boy, a tiny little girl and two grown-ups at peak 'midlife crisis' age. It was a recipe for disaster and, cooking the shit out of that disastrous recipe, we slopped mess all over Mum's precious black and white tiles.

The tiles became a symbol of Mum's struggles. She would obsess over them; we often found her scrubbing them on her hands and knees, muttering to herself about how useless everyone was. She would take it personally when anyone spilled anything on them, which, with four gross kids, happened often.

'Who walked through the kitchen with grubby shoes on?!' Mum would scream.

This became one of Mum's catchcries, a signal that she was at her wits' end, which seemed to be her favourite place to be in this phase of her life. She was in the thick fog that we now know to be menopause; at the time we just thought she was a stranger. And she was. We couldn't recognise this furious, chronically depressed woman who screamed at us like a banshee with red-wine lips. The fights between Jurek and Mum escalated and the dream house we'd waited so long to move into became the most awful place for anyone to be.

Jurek responded poorly to Mum's mental snap by doing things that intentionally pissed her off. Like going for a bushwalk with Rosie and then walking his muddy shoes all the way through the house, including over her black and white tiles. Mum, who was always on the brink of crumbling and often propped herself up with Nescafé and curt apologies for her atrocious behaviour the night before, saw these muddy footprints as a personal attack. She screamed and screamed and screamed, and we pushed ourselves back into darker corners of the house, waiting for her to run out of steam. Jurek would rise to the challenge and scream back, but we kids knew better than to get involved. There was no way of stopping their fights, so we would just have to wait quietly until she was silent – still furious, of course, but silent fury is just that *tiny bit* easier to live with.

I missed Hamish wildly, but tried to focus on how great the new house was aesthetically. I dreamed of the day I could bring high school friends over and act like our built-in deep fryer was no big deal and that we definitely didn't squeal with delight for days when we learnt about it. Surely now that I was in this house, the worst of my issues were over – I could finally feel like I belonged at that school. But I never did. The house may have looked lovely, but Mum and Jurek, who'd both worked so hard to make it happen, had never been more miserable. It made no sense to us kids. It took a while for me to realise I had no control over Mum's moods, but I wanted to show my friends I mattered now, so at the ripe old age of fourteen, I ran a risk and invited two of them for a sleepover.

This invitation was huge for me. I hadn't had anyone round for a sleepover since primary school. I was so keen to show my high school friends just how magnificent our new home was. We slept downstairs in the big lounge room because I was still sharing a room with my bully/sister Amy, and I wanted to be as far away from Mum and Jurek as possible just in case they missed the memo that I was pretending to live in a normal, happy household. I proudly showed my friends around and they were polite enough to not point out my feigned nonchalance. We had a great time ... until we didn't.

It was a dangerous move to invite my friends over during this time, but I thought Mum and Jurek would be able to see just how important this night was for me. At the start, it was excellent – Mum was viscerally happy and kept throwing her arms around my friends, telling them how beautiful they were. She was magnetic and funny, and my friends gushed about how lucky I was to have such a fun mum. Jurek was also in fine form – he ordered pizzas and made Mum laugh until she was holding on to the kitchen bench to stay upright. I was ecstatic! If this is what it took to bring some happy vibes into our house, I would have sleepovers every night! After their first few drinks disappeared, Mum and Jurek decided to take themselves to the Roo's Club, which made my stomach do a nervous flip. You'd never know how they'd return after a boozy visit to the Kangaroo's Club, but I held on to my optimism like a kid on the last rung of the monkey bars. I figured if they had been so good so far, surely they could keep the ruse up for twelve more hours. Surely!

We were woken at 2am to the sound of Mum and Jurek screaming. My whole body tightened and filled with icy dread. I squeezed my eyes shut, pretending I was asleep, hoping I was the only person who could hear them. Then I heard my friends whispering to each other about whether they should call their parents to pick them up, and I wanted to die.

Mum and Jurek yelled at each other for hours, slamming doors and storming noisily across the floorboards above us. They'd fucked it and I had never hated them more in my life. I tried to tell my friends that this never usually happens and they would go to bed soon, but they once again made a liar out of me. For hours I made jokes to distract my friends, and they giggled through their worry, making mental notes to never come back to this house again. And I didn't blame them for that. I certainly didn't want to be there.

Once the screaming faded, we finally went back to sleep. A few hours later, I woke with a knot in my stomach to the sound of my mum scrubbing the black and white tiles. She wasn't muttering furiously this time; she must have run out of hateful words after the night of screaming. But those hateful words rang in our ears as we packed up our makeshift beds and talked quietly about what to make for breakfast. I seethed at how Mum was tending to those tiles when the real mess – me – was downstairs, fighting back angry tears as she tried to make her friends laugh.

My friends never did come over for another sleepover. I never asked them to. The damage was done, the lesson learnt: the sleepovers were over.

We know now that our sinking ship was caused by Mum's menopause, and it was exacerbated by how ill-equipped we all were to handle it. Menopause was cruel to my mother and, as a result, it was cruel to the whole family. We lived with a woman we didn't recognise – an angry, bitter, miserable woman who'd replaced our kind, joyous warm mum, and we missed her ferociously. We all responded differently to this new woman – Jurek antagonised her, Hamish ran from her, Amy avoided her, Simon defended her, Rosie held her and I hated her with my whole being. How dare she take my mum away when I needed her so much? Was this the price we had to pay for this fancy new home? If so, it was a shit deal.

For a long time I'd thought all I wanted was a nice house like my posh friends had, but it turned out that all I really wanted was my mum. I can't even imagine how scary that time was for her – to be in a mind and body she no longer understood. Part of me wishes I could go back in time, hug her and tell her that it was all temporary, but at the same time, I never want to see that woman again.

Mum did come back to us – not entirely, but mostly. Menopause chipped something sparkly out of her and left her incomplete and remorseful. I wonder if it would have been different if she'd known what was happening to her, if we all knew it wasn't actually about the fucking black and white tiles. The secrecy that surrounded menopause, especially back then, destroyed so many women's lives and imploded entire families – so many disasters that could have been prevented with a little bit of awareness.

Mum sold our house recently, after twenty-two years. While it was definitely a gorgeous house, it was the keeper of some of the worst years of my life and I won't miss a single thing about it, not even the deep fryer.

WE ARE ALL TURNING INTO OUR MOTHERS

'Gosh you look like your mother, Bronnie!' beamed my aunty Di. She held my eleven-year-old face in her hands. I didn't think I looked anything like my mother. Helen had beautiful, bronzed skin, big brown eyes, auburn hair thanks to her trusty box dyes and a slight frame, whereas I had fair skin, dark blonde hair and green eyes and was often referred to as a 'solid girl' by the older generation, who struggled to talk to a female without describing their body to them. I blushed and looked at Mum, who was instantly up herself about the comment.

'She does look like me. She doesn't look a bit like her dad, does she?' she asked proudly. I didn't admit it, but I was thrilled to be compared to my mum. I grew up thinking she was the most beautiful woman on the face of the earth (well, at least the most beautiful woman in Belconnen, ACT – *easily*).

It wasn't until I hit my teenage years that this comparison became the last thing I wanted, and that's nothing against Hels – every girl fears it. We are all fucking petrified of turning into our mothers. It doesn't matter how much you fight it, you always find yourself slowly developing her mannerisms, mimicking her laugh and leaning into her quirks. Even if you have the best mum in the whole world, and you're one of those insufferable people who say, 'My mum is my bestie', you would still scoff at the thought of becoming her. It knocks the wind out of you to notice yourself reading signs aloud to people who can definitely read, or fluffing when you sneeze, or – the most confronting one of all – rousing on your kids the way she used to rouse on you – which you promised yourself, when you were a kid, you would never ever do.

This will be relatable if you've screamed any of these down the hallway:

'If I have to pick up these shoes one more time, I will throw them in the bin!'

'Am I speaking to no one?!'

'I guess I'll unstack the dishwasher, shall I?'

'I don't know where your netball skirt is! I've never worn it!'

Or my mum's favourite:

'Criticise, criticise, criticise! That's all you bloody kids ever do!'

Now, I haven't said the last one yet, but my kids are still small enough to think I'm the greatest woman alive, so it's on the backburner, I'm bloody sure of it.

I am turning into Helen. As magnificent as she is, the thought is very sobering. I think we're scared of turning into our mothers because we spent our teenage years and early twenties muttering 'She is mental.' It takes years to shift the tone of those mutterings from impatient to endearing. For me, it was when I became a mother myself. I reckon I had the least patience with Mum out of all her kids when we were teenagers. It felt like she was *trying* to annoy me, and honestly I am still not convinced otherwise. She breastfed my little sister, Rosie, until she was almost five years old, which meant I was fifteen, with fifteen-year-old friends who had to see a giant child, with the ability to eat a T-bone steak, lift my forty-six-year-old mother's shirt and suck on her forty-six-year-old boobs. Un-fucking-forgivable.

Breastfeeding wasn't as smooth sailing or as hard to give up for me as it was for Hels, but the older I get, the more I realise I'm turning into her. I've noticed I'm becoming more and more defensive of my country background as I get older; Mum is the proudest Riverina woman you'll ever meet. She will tell everyone she's from Coolamon, a rural town near Wagga Wagga, and no one has ever asked. She'll tell waitresses, tram drivers, strangers on the street. She'll make it wildly obvious she isn't from the 'big smoke' by littering her vernacular with quintessential Australian sayings – my mum's favourite flavour of sayings. If someone talked too much, they 'could talk the leg off a wooden chair', and when an extra person came for dinner, she'd laugh and say, 'I'd better throw another bucket of water in the soup!' Even though she never made soup – we only ever ate spaghetti bolognaise that she'd make in a vat at the start of the week and would be our dinner every single night. It was delicious.

Being from Coolamon is an enormous part of Mum's identity. For a long time I thought her constant references to the tiny town were from a place of nostalgia, but I've since learnt she hates the place. Growing up in a small town sounds nice enough, but growing up in a country town in the 50s and 60s as a girl who never felt like she belonged would have been terrible. The way Mum describes it, everyone knew everyone else's business better than they knew their own. She said she was always envious of the boys in the town because being a girl back then was bloody awful. This makes sense to me – there are still plenty of mysteries surrounding female anatomy (have there been any studies into endometriosis yet, or are those women witches? I can't remember), so it pains me to think about how confusing it would have been to go through puberty in an era in which girls thought they were dying when they got their first period.

The theory that we turn into our mothers is new for me. I certainly didn't see any similarities between my mum and my nan when I was a kid. Nan was a God-fearing, chocolate-slice-baking granny who looked like an old woman from the age of forty, whereas mum was effortlessly beautiful, hated cooking and smoked loads. I honestly can't believe they were even related.

Nan featured a lot in my upbringing. We grandkids schlepped our way on a Greyhound bus from Canberra to Coolamon to spend all of our school holidays in her cosy mudbrick home, which always smelled like fried, crumbed lamb cutlets or freshly baked scones. Nan would schlep to Canberra to help Mum raise her (then only) four kids, a task she was doing alone. Dad lived in Coolamon, but unfortunately it took him too long to find a way to fit into our lives – but that's a story for another day. Nan was our second parent when he didn't know how to be, and I don't know how we would have survived without her.

She would sleep in one of the bottom bunks with either my little brother Simon or me and, even though her hands were like blocks of ice, we always fought over who got to sleep with her. She would tell us stories about growing up with five sisters, and how handsome Pop was and how much of a shame it was that he died before we got to meet him. I don't think I've ever met a couple who loved each other as much as my nan and pop loved each other, and I wasn't even there to witness it – she just described their life together so beautifully that, even though I didn't know him, my heart missed him too. We could listen to Nan tell the same story over and over and over again, which was lucky because she had about ten on rotation. She would cover her mouth as she giggled through telling them and even if we didn't understand why that part of the story was funny, we laughed because she was laughing. She was joy in human form, that woman, which is why it made no sense when Mum said Nan wasn't always like that.

Mum was always a bit weird about Nan. It was confusing for us kids because Nan was the sweetest old lady alive, and Mum seemed to freeze up when we gushed about how warm and wonderful she was. After a few wines Mum would say things like, 'Nan is a lovely nan to you, but she was a really hard mum to me.' I thought she must have been making it up because *as if* my nan could be mean to anyone. It wasn't until I had kids of my own that I understood the difference one generation can make to a mother. Mum is a better grandmother than she was a mother. She's a better mother to me now that she's become a grandmother, and I'm a better daughter since becoming a mother. I don't really know how to explain that, but I think adding a cuter, more vulnerable generation below us softened us both.

Now that Nan is gone and Mum is a grandmother herself, there are tiny things she does that remind me of Nan. She loves her grandkids as much as Nan loved us, she tells the same story often, and she giggles at everything her grandkids say. She may be turning into her mother in the best possible ways, but not entirely. She still smokes like a chimney; some things will never change. Benson and Hedges Extra Smooth represent! Hels loves her darts, maybe because they're the only filter she has.

I know I'll love becoming a nan myself because not only will I have more time for the grandkids than I did my own kids, but by then I'll truly understand how quickly they grow up. I'll have seen it happen with my own kids and lived to regret hurrying it all along. I'm in the chapter of my life when my kids look the same all of the time, but when I look at photos from only a year ago, I think, 'Oh my god, they were tiny!' It's heartbreaking to think I'll miss this time in my life when I spend 90 per cent of it feeling overwhelmed. I wish I was better at slowing down. (Self-) criticise, (self-)criticise, (self-)criticise, that's all I bloody do.

MUM'S MENTAL SMASH

I'm certain I'm turning into my mother because not only am I using one of her favourite sayings, 'If you do that one more time, I'll hit the roof!', but I actually hit the roof like she did. Allow me to explain what 'hitting the roof' is because I once had an American lady in my audience who didn't know what it was, and when I asked her to guess, she said, 'Is it smoking weed?' I had to explain that it isn't a chemically enhanced high, it feels better way better than any drug, but the comedown is much worse.

Okay, for those who don't know what 'hitting the roof' is, it's when you reach your wits' end, or have 'had it up to here!' (another one of Hels's faves) and all the pent-up rage bursts out of you like a fiery explosion and you cannot stop until the rage has reached every wall of your home. You may never have hit the roof before, but I'd bet my bottom dollar that your mum hit it at least once. It's a bit scary at the time, sure, but as a kid, it's bloody liberating to see your mum go ballistic and say words she never usually says, words that you'll forget almost instantly and she'll regret as she lies awake at night. It's fun for the whole family!

Hels was a single mother of four, then after Jurek died of cancer when Rosie was only ten, she became a single mother of five. Considering she had so many bloody kids, it is kind of surprising she didn't hit the roof more often, but it takes energy, so I reckon if she wasn't so tired, she would have. As a mother myself, I now know what reaction she wanted from us when she hit said roof. She would have wanted us to look at her remorsefully and sympathetically, and say, 'Oh my goodness, we are so sorry we did that. You have sacrificed so much for us – your mind, body, social life, soul – and we have taken advantage of you. We are so sorry. How can we fix this?'

But you don't say that when you're a kid, because when your mum hits the roof, it's the funniest thing you've ever seen. You have to stifle your giggles and, as soon as you can, you run to your siblings and whisper, 'I saw a vein pop out of her neck that time!'

I used to think when Mum hit the roof, it came out of nowhere. Like she was perfectly content, and then BAM! What a tiny moron I was. However, I have learnt that sometimes it does come out of nowhere. Only recently, I saw my middle child (aged eight) standing next to her shoes in the lounge room and said, 'Hey mate, can you pick those up?' I felt fine. Serene, even. And then she said, 'What?'

I saw white. I exploded. 'I said, pick up those bloody shoes!' She looked at me like my head was spinning and pea and ham soup was spilling out of my mouth. I put myself in timeout for that one. Even mums need the timeout corner sometimes.

The best time my mum hit the roof, the most *epic* hitting of the roof, was when all of us kids were teenagers or almost teenagers. Mum was going through the hot-flush-fury stage of her life, and we had absolutely no idea what was happening to her, but we were the kids, and she was the mum, so it wasn't our job to work it out – it was hers. I reckon those hot flushes cooked a lot of our meals – no heating elements were required at that point of her life, she would just stuff a raw leg of ham up her Sussan's blouse and dinner was cooked in no time.

Mum was furious from the moment she came home from work on this particular day, which wasn't an unusual state for her since we moved into our big, flash house. We thought the move would make her happy, but it seemed to have had the opposite effect and, as none of us had any idea what was happening and she never offered an explanation, we just bit our tongues and hoped she would be happy soon. She wasn't.

The temperature changed as soon as she walked in the door and we knew better than to ask her if she was okay. We just had to get out of her way unless we wanted her black mood to spill all over us. She poured herself a large glass of red wine, the first of many for the night, and started bashing around in the kitchen muttering to herself about how useless everyone was and how no one ever helped her – and we didn't really help her, if I'm completely honest, but the kind of help she needed couldn't come from us.

After about an hour, she yelled out, 'DINNER!', which was bloody brilliant news because as growing kids we were absolutely starving. Food was worth the risk of a run-in with Hels – well, we thought it was. Boy oh boy, how wrong we were. If we knew what was to happen at this dinner, we would have gone to bed hungry.

All five of us trailed into the kitchen and glanced at Mum, hoping her mood might have softened under the weight of the cab sauv, but it hadn't. Her lips were tightly shut, her eyes dark and her blouse splattered in pasta sauce. If I could have gone back in time, I would have turned on my heels and walked to the servo for dinner, but I didn't know what was ahead of me. I had no idea what Mum was capable of, and neither did she.

We were all perched around the vintage glass-top dining table that Mum had bought from the Pakistani embassy when we first moved into the house. She loved this table because it was handmade with gold trimming in the carved mahogany. It clashed with the rustic kitchen and the black and white tiles it stood upon, but Mum had to have it because it suggested such affluence. She bought a lot of things to distance herself from the second-hand furniture we'd lived with in commission housing. This table, along with all the other pieces of furniture she bought, was supposed to make her happy.

We sat in stone-cold silence, hoping Mum would notice we were nervous, but it didn't change anything. Nothing we could do or say could lighten the darkness she was wading through, so we chose silence. We hoped she would look up at her five kids and choose to have a nice family dinner, but she did no such thing. Our eyes darted around the table, hoping someone would know how to ease the tension, but we all looked just as bewildered as each other. This wasn't good and, it's sad to realise, it wasn't unusual. In this chapter of her life, this was the vibe Mum brought home; it was the only vibe she could muster. She exuded a general disdain both for the life she found herself in and the children her body had borne. She was so different to the mother we'd known a few years earlier, and my heart bled for my four-year-old sister, Rosie, who was experiencing this new furious and fed-up mum at such a young age.

Mum looked over at us five giant hungry kids she'd created and her shoulders tightened. Just the sight of us seemed to make her want to scream, but she didn't. I wish she had; it would have released some of her anger, which would have been preferable to what came next. She dragged the pasta bake out of the oven, stormed over to the table she'd loved so dearly, and slammed the casserole dish down so hard that both the casserole dish and the prized table completely shattered. We all sat there holding our breath, mouths agape at the smashed glass and pasta on our adolescent thighs. She had officially lost it.

We all slowly stood up, brushed off the debris and walked out of the room. We piled into one room and mustered up the energy to giggle about it. What else could we do? We had just witnessed the hardest Helen would ever hit the roof and it was ... spectacular! It was a new record, and we all got to see it! We tried to make light of it for Rosie, but also for ourselves because, holy shit, what a bloody mess. We kids had learnt from an early age the skill of dragging humour into trying times. I don't know how healthy it is, but I'm a professional comedian now, so I guess I have to be #grateful for it somehow.

We went to bed without dinner that night, listening to Mum and Jurek scream at each other about the smashed table. He hadn't been sitting at the table with us because he was busying himself in a different room to avoid her wrath, an exercise that only made her angrier. Their fight that night was explosive. A fitting end to a fucked night.

It's been about twenty-five years since that horrific night, and we still talk about it, in the desperate hope we might colour the memory in a brighter shade. It's funny how we try to laugh about the tricky things, but I guess if we didn't, we would realise just how small we are against them. Humour is handy that way. Mum doesn't love when we bring up that night; in fact, she doesn't like talking about that time of her life much at all. She always blushes, giggles nervously and slinks outside for a ciggie. I'd be lying if I said we did it innocuously. I can't speak for my siblings, but I reckon I remind my mother of that chapter of her life as thinly veiled revenge. It sounds heartless – because it is – but it's hard to truly forgive someone who broke your heart like Mum did all those years ago. Watching someone who is supposed to protect you no matter what become the person who scares you the most is often unforgivable. Almost.

It wasn't until I lost my mind with postnatal anxiety and depression (SPOILER!) that I could even come close to understanding what Mum was going through. I now live in dread of menopause – who knows what those bloody hormones will do to me or how scared I will make my kids? Menopause, like all women's health issues, is treated as an inconvenience to society. It's like mould in a damp room – something that's annoying to deal with but, left to its own devices, will grow and destroy everything around it. However, unlike black mould, we don't really know how to deal with women's hormones so we feel victimised when someone we love is struggling with them. 'My sister is such a moody bitch now that she's pregnant, poor me!' 'My wife changed when she had our kids, poor me!' 'My mum smashed our kitchen table, poor me!'

We wait for the woman to fix herself, relying on a long history of silenced women as evidence that they will. I know that when I went mad after having my babies, I was more isolated than ever. It's awkward to call a mad woman mad, so we let her go mad, and wait patiently for her to fix herself.

What's more, we *expect* women to go mad. We tell young girls that they'll go mad any minute. At least once a week, a stranger, family member or friend will say to me, in earshot of my eight- and ten-year-old daughters, 'You've got your work cut out for you when they're teenagers', as if when they turn thirteen, they'll evolve into hateful, uncontrollable molls. (When we talk about teenage boys, we say, 'Careful, when they turn into teenagers they'll eat a lot.' Who cares! That's what Weet-Bix is for!) Then, when these teenage girls turn into women, they're told that if they don't have kids, they're crazy, and if they do have kids, they'll definitely go crazy because early motherhood is isolating and hard, and enormously confronting when you love something so much but hate the experience. And that's before you even consider menopause.

I am terrified of menopause. I am turning into Helen and she lost her footing spectacularly when she went through it. We heard people flippantly say, 'She's going through "the change"', as if she'd been stung by an insect on a weird sci-fi movie and she was morphing into a monster. And, if I'm perfectly honest, that was what it felt like: my mother, the monster. I remember her face vividly when she was going through menopause: she wavered between looking exhausted, furious and terrified. There isn't a lot of room to feel safe when your mum is visibly scared.

It's only now that I realise that when Mum threw that casserole dish through the glass dining table, and we stood up and left the room, we left her standing in the kitchen thinking, 'Oh my god, my kids have a smashed table and a broken mum, and I don't know how to fix either.'

I know why we are scared of turning into our mothers. It's because we've seen the worst of them. And not only that, we've seen them struggle as silently as possible, and that looks bloody petrifying. I am turning into Helen. I am embracing this more as I grow older, but I hope I'm kinder to myself than we were to her when menopause comes for me.

Until then, I've made a promise to myself: never ever buy a glass-topped table.

HELEN'S VERSION

I didn't think it was fair to tell so many stories about Helen without giving her the chance to give her version. So this chapter is written by Hels, my glorious mum.

The year was 1959 and the only town I had ever been in was Coolamon. Dianne Crocker, 'Crock', and I had been besties since birth, and we were excited about Gail Moore's sixth birthday party in a few days' time. We saw her dad, Knockie Moore, out on his back porch and asked him whether Gail was having chicken sandwiches at her birthday party – the very best kind of sandwiches, in our eyes. He laughed and said, 'Not unless you bring the chook!'

Broken-hearted, we walked up the back lane to my house, scaled the gate and, as we walked past the chook house, had a brilliant idea. I told Crock that there was a chook that was easy to catch 'cos she just sat there all day. We dragged the axe down from the woodheap, and one of us held the chook on the ground while the other chopped at its neck. When the axe-wielding four-year-old grew tired, we'd swap. We'd seen our dads do this so often but it was much harder than it seemed. Finally, to our astonishment, we hit it! We winced at the sight of the blood, then squealed with joy as we realised that those chicken sandwiches were on the menu! Then the chook took off with its head hanging down its side. It ran and ran like an almost headless chook, and we couldn't catch it. My father came out to see what the ruckus was about, and he was angry.

Crock scurried off as fast as her little legs could carry her. I had to bear the brunt of him carrying on about his best brooding chook. He wouldn't listen when I said we were only trying to help Gail have a good birthday, and my mother roused on me for ruining another dress. Two days later we went to Gail's party, and they did have chicken sandwiches, which we didn't eat. We were the talk of the street and ribbed by both adults and kids alike. Why is it that when I try to help, I always end up a critical mess?

Why did I remember that story when Bronnie asked me to write about my menopausal state of insanity? It's because that's how I felt during that time. I felt like a half-headless chook trying to escape the wrath of my tormenters. Back then, I was terrified of this half-headless chook, and now I was terrified of myself, as was everyone in my family. The parts of my brain that were left were the insane parts. Sanity had been severed by an axe held by two four-year-olds.

In my late forties I was losing myself increasingly each day. The morning alarm incited anger and, in my diaphoretic state, I checked my work schedule for the day. I'd spend most of the night trying to cool down on the bathroom tiles, so sleep was fitful and fraught with angry dreams. One day I had to attend five showers and three medical assessments for our community's most vulnerable people. I used to love my job – I'd found purpose in it.

I loved visiting the old people I looked after. Australia is no good at respecting our elderly, so providing people with enough dignity to see out their days in the homes they'd lovingly created over decades was so important to me. I loved the stories the most – rich tapestries of memories tied together with nostalgia. I loved it and then, suddenly, I didn't.

Old bodies with saggy thin skin, fat bellies and bums, arthritic joints, bulbous breasts, irritated and infected folds, incontinence issues, false teeth and, worst of all, long boring stories incited by loneliness. Every home that day presented me with an awful combination of these elements.

Deep breaths, deep breaths.

The sweet and caring nurse act was a hard one, but eat your heart out, Sarah Bernhardt, I put on the performance of a lifetime every blooming day! My hot flushes were uncomfortable at the best of times, but at work I had to endure showers hotter than an artesian spring and dress wounds in homes heated within an inch of their lives. Old Oga always insisted on me drying between her toes with individual tissues. Not once, but twice. Why? Who the bloody hell was going to look at them and/or check them for moisture content? Pre-menopause, I would have had a good laugh with her about this strange request, puncturing the awkwardness with humour, but I couldn't do that anymore. When she told me what she wanted and pointed at the tissues, I wanted to scream. God, I hated her that day. The externally sweet nurse was a lather of sweat. The internally irate woman was wishing, like the wounded chook, to be put out of my misery.

Right, showers done, off to the medical assessments. I asked someone if they'd had any operations.

'What, love?'

'HAVE YOU EVER HAD ANY OPERATIONS?'

'Oh, my goodness, yes. In 1945, just after the end of the war, I had my tonsils removed. It was a very risky operation back then and I almost bled out. I could have died.'

I wish you had. Abrupt, insidious and nasty thoughts shocked me. Who was I becoming?

Deep breaths, deep breaths.

Fifteen operations and one wasted hour later, I got to the next question.

Jurek and five children awaited me at home, so at the end of my working day it was off to the supermarket for tea supplies. I needed enough tucker to feed two vegetarians and five meat eaters. Pasta it is. Everyone in the supermarket was chilled out and slow. What the bloody hell was wrong with them? What did anyone have to smile about? Then there was that stupid woman at the checkout who thought it would be okay to have a long chat about how she managed to sneak vegetables into her grandkids' snacks. SHUT UP. I don't know you and I don't care about what foods your grandchildren eat after school. It took a lot of willpower not to hit her over the head with a bottle of tomato paste.

Deep breaths, deep breaths.

Eventually home, to the messiest, most uncontrolled house. The front yard a quagmire of wet clay. I'd get to it one day. A part of a car in the hallway, tools strewn everywhere, my precious black and white tiles sticky and grubby with clods of clay, the veranda with yesterday's washing draped everywhere, the kitchen sink choking with dirty dishes and pots. God, I hated this house. Take me back to my little government house in Spence, where I had a lovely garden and control. Where we were close.

Here there were windows and doors in odd places, poky bedrooms and second-hand crap everywhere.

My sanity and my children were drifting quickly away in this house I'd thought I wanted so badly. I felt powerless at the best of times and furious the rest of the time. The house was filled with life, but I couldn't see any of the kids – they were all scattered around the house, to avoid helping me. Those ungrateful little bastards never helped me. If they loved me at all, they would have lifted a finger while I was out working. No one loved me. I didn't even want their love anymore. I was finished with all of it.

Deep breaths. Deep breaths. Where to start?

A huge tumbler of wine, of course. A great tonic for a half-headless chook.

I swallowed my fury and called out to Jurek for help, but, of course, he needed to meditate. NEEDED to meditate. Bloody meditate. Where was that axe? A meditated state did remind me of a brooding chook!

So I cleaned, peeled, chopped, cooked, guzzled and sweated. I thought if my sweat dripped into the pots, then they'd taste it and understand my madness and ire. They would ingest and understand this horrible angry me. Wishful thinking.

They were all here somewhere. This house was big and had many hiding corners – unlike in Spence, where we basically sat on top of each other. Which did I prefer? The kitchen was my room, and I had loved the tiles and the cabinets and especially the table from the Pakistani embassy, which had a thick glass top over the ornate gilded wood. I needed to get everything sparkling in the hope that sanity would return, that the half-head would heal. Fat chance: by this time, I was three sheets to the wind! That vino tonic was having an adverse effect tonight.

In hindsight it always did. I was absolutely fuming.

I called them all for tea through gritted teeth and they slipped from cracks in the walls and sat at the table. My blood was boiling and from out of left field I lost it. I picked up one of the pasta dishes and threw it so hard at the table I smashed the shit out of the glass top. Glass and pasta sauce all over them and, worst of all, the black and white tiles. They all ran back to whence they came, and I sat on the floor and cried drunk, menopausal, woeful tears.

Had I severed the chook's neck? No, the half-headed chook had to clean up. The black and white tiles were in a dreadful state, but they were not alone.

I'D RATHER DROWN

I have never liked learning. In fact, I think I hate it. One of the main reasons I became a teacher was so no one would ever force me to learn again. The way I see it, a chef never eats their own food, a carpenter never finishes their own house, the police don't follow the law and a teacher never has to learn.

This explains why becoming a mother was such a shock to my system: I hadn't read anything about it before I found myself cradling my first baby. I stared blankly at the midwives in the hospital when they gave me pamphlets, which I quickly threw in the bin. I'm not sure why I hate learning – it seems like such a strange thing to hate, but even when I was a kid, I always thought I knew enough. What I have come to learn about motherhood is you never know enough about anything, ever, and, because of this, I figure why bother trying?

I attended the bare minimum of classes at university, just enough to pass. On the first day, I would trick a dumb-dumb future PE teacher into asking the lecturer what the minimum attendance rate was. It wasn't hard to spot the future PE teachers, because even though they were not, in fact, PE teachers just yet, they always, always dressed like they were.

They would wear shorts all year round, and a polar-fleece vest over a polo shirt, and a shark-tooth necklace around their thick necks. Even if you were blind, you could work out who the future PE teachers were by their names. All of the Tegans, Brodies, Shannons and Tylers had a bright future in dodgeball and awkward sex-ed lessons with teenagers. Weirdos.

I figured if I asked Brodie to ask the lecturer for the attendance rate, the lecturer would make a point of ensuring Brodie was at every class. It was a cheeky question that we all wanted to know the answer to, but only one sacrificial lamb was dim enough to ask. Come to think of it, I should have bought Brodie a new whistle as a token of my gratitude.

Once I knew the minimum classes to attend, I reluctantly attended them. I would spend the entire class or lecture counting down the minutes until I could race back to my car and leave the campus for a life where I wasn't learning a damn thing. Safe to say I was not involved in the university community whatsoever, and I had very few friends there. It's hard to make friends when you're rarely there and, when you are there, you're either manipulating the Tegans in plain sight or sprinting to the car park.

Whatever I learnt was against my will, smooshed into university essays no one would read, and then hastily forgotten. I don't know for certain that none of the university tutors read them, but I am quietly confident not many did. This is because my Gothic Literature tutor told us in no uncertain terms that he did not. He was a clichéd tortured artist, comically so, with scruffy hair, leather sewn onto the elbows of his tweed blazer, twenty-four-seven red-wine lips, a constant scowl and a foul energy born from the idea he'd been overlooked his entire life. One of my favourite memories during university was this trainwreck of a man barging into the classroom with an armful of assignments and a black coffee tilted just enough to spill ever so slightly and announcing, 'Yes, I'm late, but I didn't want to come at all.' He was a mess, and I loved him. He walked in one day, late as usual, slammed the messy pile of *Dracula* assignments on his desk and said, 'You all got seventy-five per cent. Full disclosure, I didn't read them, I don't get paid enough to teach *and* mark, so you'll have to settle for one, and here I am before you, teaching.' He then slumped into his seat and put his head in his hands, where he remained for the rest of the class. We all looked at each other, elated, except for the nerds who'd put effort into critically analysing how *Dracula* explores sexual repression, salvation and madness. Losers.

One thing I do remember learning was that children are naturally curious, and their desire to learn must be encouraged. This begged the question: if learning is naturally appealing to humans, why am I so determined to not have a bar of it? I reckon I know exactly when that urge fizzled out, and that was when I was a small child being taught to swim.

As the third-born child, my swimming lessons came later than they should have. When I was a baby, we lived across the road from the local swimming pool in a small country town, so my older brother and sister learnt how to swim as soon as they could walk. This wasn't because Mum and Dad were keen swimmers, or had strong values when it came to fitness, wellbeing or sport; they needed to learn how to swim because my older sister Amy had a death wish. By the age of two, she had grown so obsessed with the pool that she would put on her black Speedos, escape the house, walk over the wide, hot bitumen road and sneak through a small hole in the fence. It wouldn't have been hard to escape – Mum had a three-year-old and a newborn as well, and who in the world would assume they'd need to account for a rampant, suicidal two-year-old in their day-to-day? To be fair, Mum should have started factoring that in after the first ten times Amy pulled this stunt. Two-year-olds are tiny and super unreasonable, and this mission became Amy's sole purpose in life.

The pool was run by an extremely tanned lady with thin lips, a fluro pink visor and a constant cigarette that wobbled when she spoke. When Amy was successful in sneaking into the pool, the woman would have to sprint to catch her before she threw her tiny body into the deep end, where all the pimply teenagers were doing bombs. After wrangling the determined toddler into the canteen, which smelled of hot jam doughnuts – a smell that melts the skin off the roof of my mouth to even think of it – the tanned lady would sit Amy down, give her a lolly to keep her still, call my mum and say, 'She bloody got in again, Helen.'

Mum would sigh, swing me up and onto her shoulder, grab my older brother by the hand and storm over to the pool. She would apologise, and insist it wouldn't happen again, even though the super-tanned lady knew she'd see this army of lost causes again the next day, potentially even later the same afternoon.

We didn't stay in that house for much longer. We moved to a series of freezing farms where Dad worked, all with shitty houses that had no heating. Feeling cold is the only constant feature of all my early memories. I vividly remember climbing into Mum and Dad's bed in the middle of one icy-cold night to get warm. I was two, and we lived on a goat farm in Adelong, New South Wales, where it seemed eternally soggy and grey. I cuddled up to Mum as she breastfed my newborn brother and I shoved my frozen feet between her warm thighs. I went to sleep under the scratchy blankets and, when I woke up, demanded Mum sing my favourite song, Cher's 'If I Could Turn Back Time'. Mum was so used to this request that she started singing it to me with her eyes still closed. I love that memory, though now, as a mother myself, I realise I must have been unbelievably annoying and would almost certainly have woken my baby brother just to get my Cher fix. But what are you going to do, not make your exhausted mother sing Cher? I don't think so.

Toddlers have an incredible ability to block out babies. I guess it's to feel important for a few more years, which is understandable, I guess, but also bloody annoying when you're the mother of a newborn who really could do without song requests yelled into their face at 6am. If I could turn back time, I might have made my big sister sing it, but as a four-year-old she was already a bitch to me by then, so maybe I made the right decision.

The arctic farms had dams, but not swimming pools, so I went without swimming lessons until I was about three. By then, I'd moved in with my nan for a while in Coolamon. How this came about was that Mum's cousin Aunty Didy came to visit us on one of these farms and noticed how grim the situation was. Dad worked a lot or was at the pub (I don't remember him home much at all), there were now four kids aged one to six, and Mum was skinnier than she'd ever been thanks to seven years of relentless breastfeeding and not a huge budget for food. I guess it would be hard to chub up when the inside of your house is colder than the frosted paddocks around you.

Aunty Didy opened the fridge which was full of beers and not a lot of food and her heart sank. She looked out at me on the trampoline bouncing away in the frigid temperature, and then back at my exhausted mum who was ironing school uniforms and wildly embarrassed her beloved cousin could see how we were living. Mum recalls how kind Aunty Didy was in that moment, a character trait so quintessential to that woman, when Aunty Didy sat on the only couch we had and said, 'Oh, isn't this lovely, Helen?' Mum choked up trying to work out where it all went so wrong, but held back her tears because if there is one thing that ladies from the Riverina are, it's proud. Aunty Didy asked if she could take all four of us kids to my nan's house, but Hamish and Amy were already at school and Simon was still breastfed, so Mum agreed that I could go. I can't imagine how hard that conversation was for both of those women, but I know it would have been without judgement or drama – just two stoic country women solving a tiny part of a gigantic problem.

I don't remember this, but when I was thirty-four I visited Aunty Didy in Wagga Wagga and she welled up telling me how proud of me she was. I didn't really understand why – I was heavily pregnant with my third baby and I had just abandoned my teaching career, and steady income, and thrown myself into comedy, with absolutely no guarantee it would work. I brushed off the overly emotional praise for as long as I could until she told me the story of me as a tiny frozen toddler with a mum who had bitten off more than she could chew. I felt for mum in that moment. She would have been so unbelievably glad someone was offering her help, but must have felt embarrassed that she needed help at all. Since having children, I know that conflicting feeling intimately: desperately needing help, but offended when it's offered.

She told me that she watched me climb into her car and waited for me to start crying for my mum or my dad or even my siblings, but I didn't. She said I was so quiet and calm, which breaks my heart a bit. I know Mum was doing her best, but it makes me wonder just how unpleasant that home was that I was totally fine about leaving it indefinitely.

I don't know exactly how long I stayed with my nan but I know I bloody loved it: my sweet, giggly nan all to myself. Her home was always warm, and she cooked the most delicious crumbed lamb cutlets in the electric frypan, and my boofhead brothers and sister were nowhere to be seen. As the third-born of four (by this stage), this was paradise.

Nan enrolled me into the local preschool and, when summer rolled in, she sent me to swimming lessons. Oh, you thought I went off track? Well, welcome to my brain, which I have forced you all to visit for this entire book. I get to the point eventually, but I love a long story, which is just a nice way of saying I think that every single detail and backstory is required for you to fully understand even the simplest of things, and by the end of this, you'll see that I'm right (or you'll have thrown the book over the back fence in fury, screaming, 'WHAT THE HELL HAPPENED WHEN YOU LEARNT HOW TO SWIM?!').

Please relax, the swimming bit is here. And spoiler: I never learnt how to swim.

Nan enrolled me in swimming classes at the local pool, the same pool that Amy used to break into daily. Thankfully her criminal ways didn't tarnish my relationship with the extremely tanned pool lady with the wobbly cigarette, so I was allowed to visit and burn the living daylights out of my mouth on hot jam doughnuts whenever I pleased. Suck shit, Amy.

I was beyond excited about swimming lessons because I would get to play in the pool and have my very first teacher. Nan lathered my lily-white skin in sunscreen, zipped up my rashie (I would have melted without it) and walked me to the pool. I was buzzing with energy. Not only was I learning to swim, but I had Nan's attention for the whole thing, so if I had a cool jump to show her, SHE WOULD BE READY AND WILLING TO SEE IT! I SAID, SUCK SHIT, AMY!

My enthusiasm came crashing down when I saw that my very first teacher wasn't the thin-lipped, super-tanned lady with the wobbly cigarette, but a man: a big, thick red bloke with grey chest hair and a wrinkled brow. I clung to Nan and asked to just play in the baby pool, but she pushed me towards the gigantic man, so I reluctantly sat on the steps next to the other kids. They all had regular swimmers on, and they were smaller than me, but that's because they weren't the third-born out of four kids (so far), so they were having their swimming lessons at the normal time. I hated the man from the get-go, and even though he didn't say anything particularly nasty, I felt like he was there to torture us. My brain decided he was a villain from a nursery rhyme, and we would eventually all end up buried in his backyard.

I don't know why my brain decided most men were dangerous, but when the thought arose, it was impossible to change it. So my dreamy visit to Nan's became slightly problematic because once a week she would hand me over to a serial killer who could stand in a body of water I was incapable of swimming in.

His lessons were awful as well. This was 1990, and swimming instructor regulations in regional Australia would not have existed, and the lessons would have come about with someone saying, 'Yeah, I could probably teach the turds how to float.' This teacher certainly gave off this vibe. He was a no-nonsense kind of fella, and he held our heads underwater as he yelled, 'Kick, would ya! Kick!' Each and every lesson, I was certain I was going to die, which isn't really the coolest energy coming from the oldest kid in the group.

One blisteringly hot day, Nan and I walked to the pool after I reeled off endless reasons as to why I needed to give this lesson a miss. 'I think I'm blind, Nan!' or 'There are sharks in the pool, Nan, I promise!' None of the excuses worked; they only made Nan rouse on me, then quickly walk to the kitchen to giggle into a tea towel. So I went, but on this particular morning, swimming lessons were cancelled. This was obviously before mobile phones, so there was no text warning Nan. Instead, we had to find out from the thin-lipped super-tanned pool lady with a wobbly cigarette who told us the glorious news slowly, often pausing to suck on her cigarette. 'He's gone and stuffed up, Gwennie, he won't be back.'

I couldn't believe my luck and, as they were chatting away, I did tiny spins on the spot. My swimming lessons were over because the giant bloke had 'gone and stuffed up', whatever that meant. Who cares what it meant! Swimming lessons were dead at the bottom of the pool, being feasted on by the sharks I made up. See ya later, swimming lessons, I'll happily live my life without that skill! And I have. It made high school swimming carnivals a living nightmare but, other than that, it's been absolutely fine.

When we got home, I overheard Nan on the phone to one of her sisters, explaining what had happened. From what I could gather, my fairytale villain got in trouble with the police and wasn't allowed to do swimming lessons anymore. I wandered around Nan's backyard, picking up sticks and throwing them, wondering what he could have done that was so bad he couldn't work with kids anymore.

That's when the penny dropped. He was a murderer. He killed kids. I'd worked it out, I was Harriet the Spy, and I'd bloody worked it out. I

KNEW he was a bad guy – I could sense it the moment I saw his furrowed brow. Chills ran through my body at the memory of his hands on me, and I wondered if he'd ever wanted to kill me.

I never saw him again, and I figured it was because he was rotting in jail with other real-life villains. It wasn't until my thirties that I asked Mum whether she felt bad I was taught to swim by a violent criminal.

Mum said, 'What are you talking about?'

I said, 'He got in trouble with the cops, and had to stop teaching kids how to swim.'

Mum scoffed at me. 'Because he got done for drink-driving and couldn't drive into town, you silly girl.'

Oh, whoops.

He was my first-ever teacher and, while it wasn't his fault that I totally misread things, the experience did set me up to be wary of learning, and probably played a part in my distrust of blokes. The old man made the mistake of driving after a few beers at the pub, but he didn't ever actually hurt me, or any kids for that matter. He did, however, scare the absolute shit out of me, and his lessons were not only a waste of my time, but hindered my desire to learn anything ever again. In all fairness, I'm sure he was a really nice bloke – hell, I'm sure he was teaching us kids to swim for free, so I hope if he's still alive he doesn't sue me for defamation.

Failing to learn how to swim is a core memory of mine and, to my bewilderment, a memory I rehashed many times after becoming a mother: I figure because both parenthood and learning to swim backed me into a corner where I felt like I had absolutely no control in a situation that truly felt like life and death. The two experiences might look different from the outside, but they were pretty bloody similar to me: frantically trying to learn new skills that felt not only foreign but often impossible, all the while publicly drowning.

I'm not lying when I say I can't swim. I truly cannot. I mean, I can stay afloat, and for some of us, that will have to do.

HAVE YOU MET THE PILL YET?

I have a million kids but, believe me, I am no stranger to the contraceptive pill. The pill and I go way back, and we've had a rockier relationship than Ben Affleck and JLo: just call me Bronnie from the Block, and the pill the guy who only dates women with the same name (I'm not confident that will catch on, but if it does, you read it here first). If I had to do a speech at the pill's twenty-first birthday, I would say, 'Happy birthday to the girl who has touched all of our lives in some shape or form. This biatch has given me peace of mind when I really, really, really didn't want to get preggo, and I'll always be grateful that she kept my late teens and early twenties baby-free. She's been there for me in some really hard times but, if I'm honest – and for those who know me you know that two grapefruit Cruisers always bring the truth out of me *pause for laughter* – I have to say that she's actually created some really hard times. So let's raise a glass for the pill, the medicine we're grateful exists but cannot deny is truly fucked in heaps and heaps of ways. Cheers, girl!'

I was late to the pill compared to most of my friends. I remember at recess in Year 10, all the girls would whip out their wallets and pull out a sleeve of contraceptive pills to compare which one their GP had prescribed. What have you got? Yvette? Yasmin? Brenda? They all sounded like spinster aunts, and if there was one thing we teenage girls wanted, it was the promise of an empty womb for a little while longer.

It wasn't only to prevent babies, though – everyone seemed to be on the pill for some reason or another. It felt like any problem a teenage girl had, the GP threw the contraceptive pill at her. Bad skin? The pill. Chubby? The pill. Moody? The pill. Inconsistent periods, even though you've only just started them and god forbid your body is working out what the fuck is going on? The pill. Having sex? The pill. Hungry? The pill. Don't have a dick? The pill.

There were no conversations about how the pill actually worked. None. We were taught not to question magic, so we just swallowed the pill and hoped we would all soon be rid of acne, love handles and pregnancy threats. There were so many different types, and so many different reasons to be on it that the pill became normal. The problem with this wide net was that it was really anyone's guess how your body would react. It was like a deranged game of Russian roulette, but instead of a bullet to the head, you might be transformed physically and mentally into a shadow of yourself. A bullet to the head would have been preferable to the roller-coaster some girls went on. One friend went on the pill, and it made her lose weight and double the size of her boobs, which was obviously the jackpot result. When she told us this, another one of our friends instantly rang her GP and was prescribed the same pill. Months later, she announced that it hadn't had the same effect: she'd put on weight everywhere *except* her boobs. What a cruel twist. This taught me two things: life is unfair, and GPs will give the pill to anyone who asks for it. Well, the non-religious GPs, anyway.

This was 2003 in Canberra, the time when about half the GPs around refused to prescribe it because #jesus. Holy hell, as I re-read that sentence, I've made it seem like 2003 was the olden days, when women couldn't vote and the streets were full of horses and carriages. There were no horses or carriages, and women could vote, but we still felt like our voices were weaker, and that's because they were. We were told in little ways all of the time that our voices were meaningless and our bodies didn't belong to us. It felt like the peak moment of teenage girls being chastised for being 'frigid' or being a 'slut'. Finding the middle ground was the 2003 version of trying to guess what fucked-up thing Donald Trump is going to say next.

We all had our reasons for taking the pill, and mine was so I could avoid having to take the morning-after pill again. I learnt the hard way that condoms weren't as trustworthy as the packet suggested, and I hated relying on someone else to make sure my womb stayed vacant, especially a teenage boy. They shouldn't be trusted with anything.

When I was seventeen, and with my very first real boyfriend, the condom broke, which was one of the scariest moments of my life. As soon as I realised, I ran a bath and jumped in, hoping to wash out the mistake, which is kind of like trying to put stockings over trousers. Logic settled in, and my first boyfriend and I drove to a late-night medical clinic to get the prescription for the morning-after pill, a relatively new medicine available to unlucky ~~sluts~~ people like myself. It wasn't over the counter in the early 2000s – you had to see a GP, which was the extra unnecessary mile ~~sluts~~ women walked to remain unpregnant.

My first boyfriend and I walked through the sliding doors of the suburban medical centre and bashfully asked to see a doctor. The waiting room was crowded with coughing and spluttering people, and the nature of the acoustics meant that everything you said to the hostile receptionist was audible to everyone else there. We whispered we needed to see a doctor, and when she said, 'Why?' I panicked and said, 'I have really bad diarrhoea,' which was gross enough for her to stop quizzing me. Sidenote: I recommend using the squirts as an excuse for any event you want to get out of. Nothing shuts down a situation faster than the threat of hot, rancid shit exploding out the leg of your jeans. You're very welcome.

We sat down, and I felt like everyone was staring at me with judgemental eyes. I felt both sheepish that I'd tried to bathe myself out of this mishap and, annoyingly, solely responsible for us sitting there. His body wasn't in danger of multiplying, so the fact he was sitting next to me made me think he was the kindest bloke alive. It's astounding how the bare minimum seems impressive when it comes to men. This deep gratitude in the sterile medical clinic is one of my most visceral moments of gendered expectation. I wish it was my last, but we all know it wasn't.

I looked around the room at the paintings above people's heads, trying to act like a woman with a non-sexual medical issue, when my eyes landed on a sign above the receptionist and my heart dropped into my guts. It read, *If you are wanting to see the doctor for the morning-after pill, these doctors will refuse it based on their personal beliefs*, which translates to: 'The following self-righteous doctors are pro-life, so fuck off and have a baby the way God intended.' The extensive list of names that followed was almost all of the doctors who worked there, which filled my body with dread. Fuck.

I nudged my boyfriend and subtly gestured towards it. He smiled and said, 'Oh, let's ask!' And it was then that I realised he harboured absolutely no shame whatsoever about the situation we found ourselves in, while I was wading in a thick muck of it. I tentatively walked to the desk and whispered, 'Am I seeing any of those doctors?'

To which the cantankerous receptionist responded loudly, 'What? I can't hear you!'

Hot with humiliation, I pointed at the sign and said, 'Those doctors. I need to see someone who *isn't* on that list.'

She swung her squeaky office chair around to look at what I was pointing at, raised her eyebrows and said, 'Oh… No, you're seeing a different one. Must be your lucky day.'

A tiny twinge of relief softened my tense shoulders before I turned to see the entire waiting room staring at me with knowing eyes, as if I had just farted in a packed elevator, but in this analogy, the fart is sperm and the elevator is my uterus. Look, not all analogies are good, especially when rifling through some of the more traumatic corners of my brain. The point is, I felt like a big ol' floozy and I wanted the ground to open up and swallow me whole. My boyfriend felt, I don't know, hungry? Nothing? Unaffected?

When I saw the doctor, he asked me some of the most confronting and invasive questions I've ever been asked. Because this line of questioning was coming from a man, I blacked out for most of it, but I'll never forget the feeling it gave me. The experience was too uncomfortable for me to hold on to, even as a bad memory. While I can't remember what he said, I do remember his visceral disappointment in me, and I remember thinking, 'I am never going to find myself in this situation ever again. Fuck this.' Little did I know it was the first of many disempowering moments I would have with the medical world and the body I lived with.

So instead of an emergency pill, I opted for a daily pill to prevent that excruciating level of shame. While everyone in high school was on the pill, acquiring said pill wasn't without its hurdles.

One of my core memories is going to the 'Family Planning Centre' in Canberra's CBD, which was where most teenage girls got the pill. We teenage girls would have to walk into a building in the centre of the bloody city, with a gigantic sign on it saying 'Family Planning Centre', and try to look inconspicuous. It was entirely our responsibility to remain childless, and to do this we had to admit to the whole city that we were horny little beasts with part-time jobs that paid enough for contraception. The name, though: I mean, come on! It's like calling a vegetarian restaurant 'Tripe and Liver'. A family? This was exactly what we were planning *against,* as randy teenagers wanting to have sex with the loves of our lives* without becoming teenage mothers.

I remember being seventeen and tentatively walking towards the Family Planning Centre, holding my breath. The year was 2003, so naturally I was wearing leggings with a top that finished just below my bum, decorated by a thick, useless leather belt that rested low on my hips. I walked quickly in my cheap ballet flats, hoping that no one I knew would see me and yell, 'Bron? Is that you? Are you ... planning a family?' Relief washed over me as soon as I walked through the glass sliding doors: I'd made it inside, seemingly unnoticed! The relief quickly dissipated when I looked around the cold, clinical room with a receptionist looking at me over her glasses. I immediately wanted to blurt out, 'Whoops! Sorry, wrong room, I'm looking for Kingsley's Chicken.' But I didn't. I needed this pill – I desperately didn't want to have an abortion and I imagined the people who worked in the abortion shop would have been even worse. You would be admitting not only that you

* They were not the loves of our lives.

were having sex, but also that you didn't know the consequences. No, thank you very much, I'd rather shit myself in public.

The stern receptionist looked me up and down, and I found myself holding my breath. I regretted not wearing more mature clothing – maybe I should come back in a three-piece suit? I knew she was judging me, which is wild because surely she saw ~~sluts~~ terrified teenage girls all day every day. Surely I was only one of the many sluts terrified teenagers trying to hold on to a sliver of control over her own body? But the way this receptionist looked at me shot fear into my soul that I was the only ~~slut~~ terrified teenager she'd ever seen in her life. I wanted to turn on my heels and run but, alas, *I had come this far* and I figured the only thing more painful than this experience was childbirth, so I approached the desk and asked to see the doctor.

The doctor was a nice enough lady, with white capris and a lipless smile. I was relieved I got a female doctor, because another male doctor discussing my fertility would have made me vomit down my front from humiliation. The relief was short-lived when I realised women can be just as self-righteous as men. It irked me that she acted like she was doing me a massive favour, and her complimenting my 'trendy fashion' made me want to set myself on fire. But *I had come this far*, so I needed to just get through whatever gauntlet she had set so I could carry on being a childless, abortionless ~~slut~~ terrified teenager.

Just when I thought I could barely stomach another second of the shameful appointment, her line of questioning kicked off. It was wildly invasive and disgustingly familiar. She asked questions I hope no one ever asks me again, and questions I hope they have refined, or scrapped altogether. They were, I realise, the same questions the male doctor asked me, which I'd buried deep in a dark corner of my psyche. It's been over twenty years since this time of my life, and the more time that passes, the more confused I am that they were asked in the first place. I was seventeen years old and just wanted the contraceptive pill – I don't know what answer I could have given that might have compromised my right to receive it. Things like, 'How long have you been sexually active? How many sexual partners have you had? Do your parents know you're sexually active? Do both parents know? How do your parents feel about you being sexually active? Are they okay about you taking the contraceptive pill? How often are you having sex? How are you finding it?'

Sure, some of those questions seemed medically relevant, but I was a teenager and embarrassed about my natural urges, so these questions felt like she was pouring buckets of hot shame all over me. It all felt so patronising and unnecessarily invasive. I was months off being able to vote on the future of the nation, and I was being asked how my dad felt about me going on the pill. I had a licence to drive a car but still had to reveal to a medical professional whether my mother was chill about me having sex. Would it matter if they weren't? When exactly do ~~sluts~~ terrified teenagers acquire ownership of their own bodies? In this current political climate, I am reminded that maybe we never do, which is a sobering thought. And so my on-off relationship with the contraceptive pill began, and with it came a medley of discerning doctors. Never once have I felt comfortable asking for, or filling, a prescription for the pill, no matter my age, mood or reason. It disappoints me immensely that more than twenty years have passed since my seventeen-year-old self tried to claim bodily autonomy, and I'd still feel shame asking to go on the pill.

But I wouldn't ask. Because the last time I did, it almost cost me everything.

Lukasz and I had become serious, so the natural progression was to go on the pill. We were still so new, so when my brain started to slip into depression so suffocating I found myself having suicidal ideation. I stifled the external signs of it because I didn't want Lukasz to think his new girlfriend was anything but a ray of sunshine, but one night I grew so terrified of the dark thoughts accosting me, that I sheepishly let him in. He, like always, wrapped his arms around me and told me that we would get through it. I was so embarrassed that this was happening to me, to us, in what was supposed to be the happiest part of our relationship. It made no sense, which depression rarely does. The next day, I went to the doctor where I explained how I was feeling. Her first question was, 'Have you recently started taking the oral contraceptive? If so, stop it. You have not responded well to it.'

I was aghast. The pill could make you suicidal? Where was the warning? 'But, I didn't know this was a side effect. Is this common?' I asked.

'Very common. It impacts your hormones, which can impact the chemicals in your brain.' She acted like she told someone this every single day of her life, and I was sitting there shocked to the core that there wasn't a warning on the packed in big bold letters that read: 'YOU PROBABLY WON'T GET PREGNANT IF YOU TAKE THESE PILLS, BUT YOU MIGHT NECK YOURSELF. YOU DECIDE WHICH ONE IS WORSE.' And that was the last time I ever took the pill.

'So cheers to the pill for giving us a sense of control, but shame on you, birthday girl, for turning our worlds upside down just when we thought we could trust you. I can't stay mad at you for the plot twists you threw my way, but I can't ever forgive you for the time you sent me mad. To the pill!'

LUKASZ, BRACE YOURSELF

When it came to our relationship, my partner Lukasz and I moved faster than a raver doing the Melbourne shuffle. We met at the perfect time in our lives. I'd left a relationship with a nice enough bloke who was too young for me and didn't think I was funny (red flag), and Lukasz had been on a string of bad first dates with women who weren't interested in what he had to offer. Huge mistake, ladies! Huge!

We met for the first time when I was still dating the Young Fella. (Eighteen months younger than me, I should add – not a child. Still, eighteen months can feel like a million years if the woman is twenty-five and the guy is twenty-three. So I guess I was dating a child? Shame on me.) The Young Fella and I had just been out for dinner, and we went to see our friend Gabe DJ at a shitty bar in Richmond. Lukasz was Gabe's new housemate, and he was sitting out the front of the bar, slumped in his chair, stoned and chatty. He looked up at me and the Young Fella and said, 'Wow! You two are a very attractive couple!' We smiled, pretended it wasn't the only thing we wanted people to think about us (we were twenty-three and twenty-five, of course that's all we wanted people to think about us), and concluded he must be from somewhere rural.

We weren't wrong. Turns out Lukasz was from a tiny country town in Queensland called Brisbane (I hope I got the spelling right there), and he'd just moved to Melbourne for work. We didn't chat with him for long, but laughed on the way home about the stoned guy who was too frivolous with his compliments for Melbourne. I said, 'That guy is going to get eaten alive!'

Months passed, and my relationship with the Young Fella came to a fiery end after he started sending me very mixed messages. He got a giant tattoo of me on his chest and about a week later almost certainly hooked up with someone else. For the record, I do not recommend doing either of these things. The breakup was dramatic and it stung for weeks, which was more annoying than anything. Finally, in an attempt to distract myself from heartbreak I ended up in a filthy bar with friends watching a band. Have I mentioned I live in Melbourne yet? Anyway, I spotted Lukasz from across the bar and the vision stunned me. He was wearing a business suit, and he could keep his eyes open. I don't want to say it's easy to impress a woman, but it turns out all he needed to do was not be ripped out of his mind and I was willing to throw a leg over. I believe the saying in France is 'va-va-voom'.

I chatted with him, and he could not get away from me fast enough. I was torn between disappointment and relief – I wanted to learn more about him, but his breath smelled like he'd just eaten an entire raw onion like an apple (Lukasz, please, there is only one Tony Abbott). Va-va-gross.

The next time I saw Lukasz was at a mutual friend's thirtieth. The nickname we had given her was Jerry Cuntfart – a nickname we loved and she tolerated, bless her. Look, if we were allowed to choose our own nicknames, the world would be a boring place. Jerry Cuntfart chose a spring races theme for her thirtieth, and we had just enough fascinators to get involved. (By the way, that nickname didn't stick: she got married, so her nickname evolved into Jerry Clithands). Jerry Cuntfart had a great nickname, and an even better thirtieth celebration because Lukasz was there in a suit again, but this time he hadn't eaten an onion on the way over. What a dreamboat! Va-va-phew!

We unashamedly pashed like teenagers at a blue-light disco, for hours and hours and hours. It was especially cringey because we started at 7pm when we were the only two on the dance floor. What desperados. Finally we sat down to catch our breath, and maybe learn each other's last names, and he showed me his (settle down, I'm a prude) keyring, which said, *I just completed the Melbourne Marathon!* You're kidding me. He's rich enough to own a suit *and* he's fit? Okay, maybe I'm as basic as they come but, like an overpriced, asbestos-riddled house in Brunswick, I was sold.

We started dating the very next day and became inseparable. He laughed heartily at my jokes, and I felt lucky to be sitting with him. It was the change we were both looking for! A budding romance that cascaded quickly into the best summer I'd ever had, apart from the summers of 1991–1997, when my siblings and I went to Narrandera pool, the best pool in the entire world. (Please don't argue with me on this, I have done extensive research. Back then the Narrandera pool had two water slides, both legitimately unsafe. You'll never feel more alive than going down the steep one because I don't think I've ever felt closer to death – ten out of ten recommend.)

It surprised absolutely no one when Lukasz and I moved in together very soon after we started dating. I mean, we basically went straight from Jerry Cuntfart's dance floor to domesticated bliss, and it felt excellent.

We moved into a teeny-tiny one-bedroom apartment in Brunswick that only had room for a bed and a couch, which felt more than enough. It didn't matter: share houses were a thing of the past; we were shacked up and LOVING IT!

I often think back to that honeymoon stage. It was completely intoxicating. We were both so enamoured with everything about each other that even the things that would grow to annoy the shit out of us seemed cute. You know, little things like, WHY DO YOU PAT YOUR CEREAL WITH THE BACK OF THE SPOON LIKE THAT? JUST EAT IT, NOT EVERY SINGLE PIECE OF CEREAL NEEDS TO BE WET! For example.

The early days were bliss because we both felt so adored. I don't think we talk about that enough. All love stories are spun from the angle of 'LOVING SOMEONE', rather than 'BEING LOVED', but they both feel just as good. It felt like everything I did was either loveable or hilarious, which was the exact opposite of how I felt in my relationship with the Young Fella. I wondered what I would have to do to look at me differently and, *trust me*, over the past thirteen years, I have shown him some really unattractive sides of me.

Only two months after the dance-floor pash at Jerry Cuntfart's party, we found ourselves on a holiday in Sri Lanka. The first couple of days were absolutely glorious and I felt like we were on an episode of *Getaway* but with fewer cameras and less money, and more beer and unbridled affection. We were shamelessly and revoltingly in love.

Then came New Year's Eve. We were at a beachside town riddled with loved-up couples tinged with sunburn and fear of the squirts. It was warm and the beers were cheap, which is where I discovered the first red flag:

I didn't feel like beer. Now, anyone who knows me knows I could drink a beer at any given time of any given day. If it's sunny and I don't have to drive anywhere, a beer is definitely on the cards. No one in Sri Lanka was asking me to operate their vehicle and the sun was in full force, so when Lukasz suggested a beer and my stomach turned, I knew something was awry. And I was right.

I tried to ignore the fact that my glands were swollen and my head throbbed because, for fuck's sake, it was New Year's Eve and I was on an international bloody holiday – this was NOT the time to get sick. I reluctantly accepted the beer and it went down like razor blades. As the afternoon progressed, I couldn't keep the charade up, so I left Lukasz at the beach with some new friends and went back to the hotel room to sleep it off.

My night was filled with feverish nightmares and, when I woke in the morning with Lukasz next to me, I was drenched. I thought it was sweat until I smelled it and realised I had actually pissed the bed. Yep, I had done a big old wee all over the mattress and all over Lukasz, the man I'd convinced I was perfect. Oh, good.

When he started to stir, he patted his back and the mattress, then shot up and said, 'Oh my god, what is that?!' My head still throbbed, but my brain raced desperately to find a way out of this. I considered saying it was just sweat, or that I had spilled a drink. Hell, I even thought about blaming him. But I couldn't. It was already too embarrassing and I would only make it worse by lying, so I put my hands over my face and muffled the words I never thought I would say in my twenties: 'I wet the bed.'

He was probably disgusted, I mean, of course he was – a grown woman urinated all over him – but he didn't show it. He gave me a big hug and told me it wasn't a big deal, even though it was, because I did a wee on him. Guys, I'm not sure if I mentioned this yet, but *I did an entire piss on my new boyfriend of only two months.* Could you recover from that? I'm the strongest woman alive! (Narrator: 'She definitely has not recovered from that.')

As I was showering and cringing my heart out, I ran my teeth over my bottom lip and noticed a familiar tingle. My heart stopped ... I was getting a cold sore. NO! I'd only had one before and it was so bad that my glands turned into golf balls and my lip hung from the weight of the awful wound. I got it in my first year of teaching and every time I said the letter 'F' or 'V', my teeth would hit the cold sore and make it bleed all down my chin. I don't think any of my students could find *Romeo and Juliet* very romantic after that.

I couldn't believe it was coming back while I was on a romantic holiday with a man who, until twelve hours earlier, had seen me as the perfect specimen! It was such a cruel twist. Now I knew what it felt like to be crowned Miss Universe only for Steve Harvey to say there had been a huge mistake.

I fretted as to how to tell him what it was and why I wasn't kissing him. I said I needed a doctor as soon as possible because I was sure this epic eruption would need antibiotics. Lukasz kindly suggested that the cold sore was the reason I wet the bed, and I ran with that. Yeah, that made enough sense for both of us. Soon enough we found a doctor (maybe?) and he gave me medicine we couldn't read and I smashed it back like MDMA caps on a dance floor, all for nothing. No, worse than nothing. The cold sore exploded onto a weeping, juicy bubble on my lip, and it was impossible for people not to stare at it, or for me not to constantly lick it, so, as you can imagine, it was a HUGE turn-on for Lukasz.

I took the antibiotics so frantically that I started to walk funny because HELLO THRUSH! I'd forgotten that antibiotics did this, so not only was I a mess up top, but I was a mess down there too. OH, GOOD!

I knew I needed cream for the thrush, so I found the nearest chemist and desperately tried to explain thrush cream to three tiny Sri Lankan women behind the counter who didn't speak a word of English. There were a lot of hand gestures and finally one woman turned to the other two and said something in Sinhala and they all looked back at me, disgusted, then down at my crotch, then back at my face and one said, 'No, no, no!' and shooed me out of the shop. I don't know what she thought I had but, whatever it was, it was rank as all hell, even for chemist ladies.

I just had to ride it out. Piss, cold sore and thrush only two months into the relationship. What a catch!

The trip actually got better after that. We found the funny side pretty quickly and laughed A LOT at my misfortune. Lukasz still looked at me like I was the greatest woman on the planet, and I thought, 'Wow, maybe there isn't anything about me that would scare him away.' All of this mess was physical, though: we hadn't seen just how badly my brain would betray me.

Once we got back to Australia, we introduced each other to our families and I did that thing we all do when we try to downplay how bonkers our families are. I said, 'My mum is pretty full on, but she'll love you.' He said, 'MY mum is Polish.' I'd met enough Polish women in my life to know what this meant. It meant, 'My mum is *really* full on and she really loves me, her son.'

The way Lukasz spoke about his mum so affectionately made me feel at ease; you can always tell a lot about a man by how he speaks about his mother. I didn't realise at the time, but I think I subconsciously knew I needed a man who was kind and forgiving. I mean, everyone needs a partner like that, but having watched my mum fall to bits so catastrophically, I knew I *really* needed one. We all turn into our mothers after all, right?

Our love was fierce, but it was young. I hadn't fallen to bits yet, and if my mum had taught me anything, it was that our mental health is about as unpredictable as a Rottweiler at a playground. We didn't know it yet, but my madness lay dormant like a man on a piss-soaked mattress in a Sri Lankan hotel.

PLANNING TO LOSE MY MIND

'Failing to plan is planning to fail.' I think that's the saying – I zone out when people say shit like this. It's never said, it is always *performed* by a smug twat who is desperate to say, 'I told you so', but has just enough self-awareness to know that absolutely no one likes an 'I told you so' person, but not enough to know that no one likes 'failing to plan is failing to fail' people either. I am not a planner – I live my life avoiding even the mention of plans. I am – say it with me – AVOIDANT, and plans are one of my favourite things to avoid.

I am a Type B personality through and through. Details are incredibly boring to me, as are instructions, schedules, itineraries and plans. It's all fluff. This isn't a hidden brag – I'm not going to imply that I've found a loophole that allows me to live my life without any planning whatsoever; in fact, I have stuffed up many, many things with my distaste for details. This aversion to a predictable day, week, year has really kicked me in the fudga more than a few times, but I simply cannot find an EpiPen big enough for this allergy.

Schools are full of people who love planning, which is a good thing. I'm sure a school would burn to the ground if it was staffed only with people like me. It almost doesn't make sense that I became a teacher in the first place. I think it happened partly because I just got sick of people asking what my 'plan' was, so I enrolled in whatever uni course I could get into. Unfortunately for Australia's future, almost anyone can become a teacher (trust, I've worked with some real numpties). The marks you need to get to become a teacher are so shamefully low that it should come as no surprise to anyone that kids are being taught by teachers who barely got through school themselves. Relax, I was one of those teachers, I can say it – you can't.

When I was a high school teacher, I never understood teachers who were hungry for structure. They stood out like sore thumbs: they were always obsessed with stationery and had colour-coded folders for each class. One time I overheard a colleague say, 'I always give my favourite class my favourite colour folder', and I've never felt more sorry for someone in my life. Who has a favourite class? And, more importantly, what self-respecting adult has a favourite colour? These are the kinds of people who celebrate their 'birthday month'. Cringe. For some reason these structure suckers are usually the humanities teachers, which means that there is something about regurgitating historical and geographical facts that gets Type A personalities all hot under their Gorman collars. These teachers bounced into school on the first day of term one with pastel folders and a pencil case with their initials monogrammed on it. No one is stealing your bloody pencil case, Lauren, relax.

These teachers are so mind-numbingly organised that they know exactly what they're teaching for each minute of each class for the whole bloody year. In my first year, I had to teach Year 7 Indonesian for eight long weeks, and I'm not an Indonesian woman nor am I an Indonesian man. The only thing I knew about Indonesia is that it invented cornrows for white women and children and named them 'Bali braids'. So we looked at photos of them for eight weeks, which is eight weeks I'm never getting back.

In my second year of teaching, I was assigned a Year 11 media class, which wasn't ideal because media wasn't one of my teaching methods, but – and this might surprise those living under a rock – there is a teacher shortage so sometimes teachers take subjects they aren't qualified to teach. It's almost like the profession isn't respected? Wild. Anyway, here I was teaching VCE media despite media not being a subject I took in high school, let alone when I was at uni. As I walked to my media classes, I would frantically look up the list of camera angles, lighting effects and directors I could ramble on about for the ninety long minutes I had those disinterested teenagers in front of me. Astonishingly, they all passed, so I got away with it. They must have learnt some bits and bobs from my confused rants, but the greatest lesson of all was for me: if you feign confidence, you can teach just about anything. And, thus, my teaching style of 'winging it' was born. Thankfully, I only taught English after that, which for me was easy to wing. I just had to have read the book – the rest was a piece of piss. Teaching literature, to me, was unbelievably easy. Marking the thousands of essays on the other hand, was boring as all hell. Yuck!

This lack of planning worked perfectly for me, but it also scratched my new-found itch: adrenaline. If I knew what the class was going to be about before I went in, I would become instantly bored, which is probably why I survived the early stages of comedy. You never know if you're going to have an okay gig or bomb so hard you can taste blood, which are the only two options for new comedians. It's the brutal nature of open mics that prompts so many people to give up after a few gigs. I needed close to a decade of pretending three things in front of an audience: that I knew what I was doing, that I was happy to be there and that everything was going exactly to plan. Teaching prepared me for comedy, so for that I am grateful.

It goes without saying that motherhood was another unplanned adventure, even more unplanned than the time I taught Year 8 sex education – an experience that has scarred me deeply.

The night I found out I was pregnant will forever be etched into my core memories, right alongside the time Amy hilariously fell through Mum's kitchen floor when the tiles were being redone: both life-changing moments. I had been with Lukasz for six months, and, as we've already established, we lived together because I'm impulsive. Our friends all laughed at us for moving in together so quickly because, to be perfectly honest, it reeked of disaster. We had only just met, and we were already popping our toothbrushes in the same cup next to the sink. Everyone we knew grabbed their popcorn and awaited the crumbling of this whirlwind relationship in the face of domesticated reality. But, as luck would have it, we didn't fall to bits. Our honeymoon stage was on steroids, with a backdrop of one of the most glorious summers Melbourne has ever seen, and the thrill of proving everyone wrong (which was intoxicating). It helped that he was the exact opposite of my ex-boyfriend, so I thought everything he did was adorable/hilarious/interesting.

His mother announced she would come and visit us from Brisbane, so I did whatever any new girlfriend would do – I cleaned the apartment within an inch of its life and, more importantly, riffled through the bathroom cabinet to dispose of anything that might make her think I wasn't the perfect woman for her beloved son. I chucked out my mini wax strips, because AS IF I had a moustache, the pill I had happily stopped taking since it send me balmy because you can FORGET ABOUT me having a baby for ages, my eyedrops, because there was NO WAY I was ever hungover, and hid my anti-wrinkle cream because it was IMPOSSIBLE for me to be that vain. In the midst of this mass exodus, I stumbled upon a pregnancy test I had been holding on to for years. I panicked and then laughed at the drama that would unfold if she found it. She would think, 'They can't already be trying for a child, they don't even know each other's middle names,' and she would be spot on. We certainly were not trying for a baby, so I thanked my lucky stars that I saw it before she did and restarted my search for incriminating but normal things to throw out. Then something came over me, and I pulled the test out of the bin to see what the expiration date was. It wouldn't be out of date for another month, so I figured I'd use it. Waste not, want not! I did a wee on the stick and thought about what other jobs I could do to secure his mother's admiration. A minute passed, and as I casually glanced down at the piss stick, I noticed there was a solid blue line and, next to it, a faint one.

Oh. My. God.

I stopped breathing, and stared at myself in the cabinet mirror. Thoughts ran chaotically through my mind: 'I can't be pregnant! I've never been pregnant. This doesn't happen to me. I am one of those non-pregnant girls. I am only a girl! I can't be having a baby, I am twenty-six years old! I am a baby myself!' I heard Lukasz cough from the bedroom and panicked even more. 'What will he say? We haven't had the baby talk.

Will he think I tricked him?'

He walked into the bathroom, looked at me, looked at the piss stick, lost all colour in his face and asked, 'What's that?' Stunned and in shock, I held it up to show him. He walked towards me, took the piss stick out of my hand and said, 'Is this accurate?' I clumsily told him I'd never had a positive one before, but I assumed it was. I'd been brought up to distrust Liberal voters, not pregnancy tests.

We silently brushed our teeth and went to bed. We both lay in silence until Lukasz said, 'Should we go buy another to be sure?' Before he'd even finished the sentence, I was out of bed and googling twenty-four-hour chemists in our area. At 11 pm on a Monday night, wearing pyjamas and thongs, we walked into a Sydney Road chemist and took four different brands of pregnancy tests off the shelf. The lady behind the counter looked at the pregnancy tests and said, 'That will be sixty-five dollars.' Then she scanned our blank faces for clues, and said kindly, 'I hope you get the result you're after.'

It hit us like a tonne of bricks – what was the result we were after? On the short drive home, we alternated between talking too much and not talking at all, because we both had a lot to say, but neither of us knew how to say any of it. I guzzled litres of water and waited impatiently for the urge to wee. I sat on the toilet while Lukasz stood in the bathroom doorway with a nervous smile plastered across his face. We laughed at the craziness of it all, and I lied and told him I thought the first test had expired so it had to be wrong.

Finally, the water made its way through my kidneys and I weed on the stick. I replaced the cap, held my breath and searched Lukasz's body language for any sign of frustration or disappointment at the situation we found ourselves in. The first blue line appeared, and then the second. Positive. A wry smile came over Lukasz's face, which instantly filled me with warmth. Thank fuck. Thank fucking fuck.

'I don't believe it,' I lied. 'I'll do another one!' Three more tests.

Positive.

Positive.

Positive.

Pregnant.

Pregnant.

Pregnant.

We stood barefoot in our tiny kitchen and laughed hysterically.

'We're going to be parents,' he said. 'We're going to have a baby!'

We laughed harder, and both did a spectacular job of hiding our terror that we were, in fact, going to be parents, and we were certainly going to have a baby.

I went to school the next day, to the job I'd studied four long and boring years to get. It was at the school where I'd done my teaching placement and I wanted to work there so badly that I pretended I was fine to teach media, for fuck's sake. I sat in my Year 7 drama class and zoned out as the smelly but mostly adorable twelve-year-olds practised their melodrama scenes in tiny groups. These classes were such a breeze: you'd teach them everything they needed to know in a few classes, and then you got two weeks of them working on their scenes while you feigned interest in their silly group politics. Still, it was hard for me to hear them complaining about some kid hogging the stage, or another kid always wanting to breakdance mid-scene, because I'd just learnt I was having a fucking baby.

I switched between being overwhelmingly excited and painstakingly terrified. I hadn't planned this at all, which was my trademark move, but this was obviously bigger than anything I hadn't planned before. The way I'd lived my life, avoiding structure and predictability, had allowed me to feel most comfortable in the unfamiliar but, again, this life-changing event felt almost indigestible. If I mispronounced a word from the media curriculum, I was the only one who was embarrassed. But this didn't affect just me. This unplanned venture held more weight than anything I'd ever carried, so I had to get it right.

The twelve-year-olds yelled and rolled around me, and I thought two things: I was going to have a tiny baby of my own with a man I loved with my whole heart, but, also, deep down, somewhere buried near my depleted bladder, I knew I was going to go mad. Again.

MY TIRED BRAIN

Before becoming a mother, I'd never seen exhaustion so intensely until my friend came to my house with her toddler after he'd skipped his nap. We stood in awe as he piffed one of his sandals, tugged down his pants and then ran around in circles, laughing hysterically. It was cute until he finally snapped. We're not sure what it was – maybe the temperature changed, or the clock was too loud – but something sent him right over the edge from afternoon bliss to a hellish dystopia, where he was the ultimate victim. He threw himself to the floor and wailed. His bright red, wet face made noises I'd never heard before and, as I desperately ran around the room looking for child-friendly things in my child-free home to distract him, I noticed my friend, his mother, just stared into space. She'd seen this universal shift before, and she knew she didn't stand a chance of curtailing it.

She'd given up. I wondered how many times she'd had to witness this before realising it was pointless to try to fight it. Which tantrum had severed her from the world she once knew, leaving her floating in the abyss, surrounded by stray Lego, overcooked plain pasta and muted screams? I knew from her blank expression that she was not the same person she was before kids – she was, in my eyes, officially mad now.

I snapped into problem-solving mode. 'What's wrong with him? What happened? Is he in pain? How do we fix this?' I squinted in the face of the cacophony coming from the small mess of a human.

She looked confused, as if she couldn't hear him at all. Was she a robot? Was she deaf? Did I need to call an ambulance? Or the police? Her eyebrows raised, and she smiled gently. 'He's just overtired,' she sighed. 'Happens at least once a day, usually about ...' She looked at her wristwatch, which was on upside down, so she had to contort her arm at a horrible angle to read it. 'Yeah, about now.' She looked over at him, smiled, cupped her hands around her mouth and yelled, 'Right on cue, buddy! You should have listened to me when I suggested a sleep today!' She laughed and rubbed her tired eyes. 'If I'm lucky, this will be the last time he'll do this today. Just ignore him, he'll stop when he's bored. I just have to survive until bedtime. Do you have any wine?'

Wine, yes, I had wine and, yes, I also needed wine at this point. Excited at having a job I could control, I quickly pulled two large wine glasses out of the cupboard and filled them generously with chardonnay. We both took gulps so big that we winced as if we'd just done shots of cheap tequila. Immediately the edge seemed to soften, and we both turned to watch the toddler writhe around on the ground, occasionally slowing down to pick his nose, then kicking off again.

I was bamboozled. Overtired? This seemed like an unbelievable overreaction to being knackered. When I was really zonked, sometimes I'd cry in my Corolla hatchback in the work car park, but I always kept my pants on. As I smugly topped up our wine glasses, I thought to myself, 'This kid really doesn't cope very well with being tired. When I have kids, mine won't be so melodramatic.'

Sorry, did I just hear every single mother in the whole world scoff? It's every mother's dream to watch smarmy childless people proudly declare what kind of parent they will one day be. 'I'll never let my kids watch screens at a cafe. I'll never *ever* let my child order a babycino, and if you ever see me do it, kick me!' If they end up having kids, every single one of those cocky idiots spends every bloody cent they have ever earned on iPads and babycinos. Trust me. I am one of them.

Before we had kids, Lukasz and I relished judging parents. Every childless person does it – it's the law. We are all allowed to experience the heights of pre-kid smugness so that we can feel the catastrophic fall from grace as soon as we procreate. Friends of ours who had a one-year-old couldn't meet up with us for lunch one day because it was their daughter's sleep time. We pretended we understood, and praised them for being such thoughtful parents to their lucky princess, but what we actually meant was we simply couldn't believe this tiny human had control over them, two grown adults. I think back to that day a lot, kind of like running my tongue over an ulcer in my mouth I got from neglecting to eat vegetables for a week. I was immovable with my own kids' sleep. Sleep controlled their moods, and I would trade all of my less important organs for a day with a kid who got into their car seat without arching their back because 'I no like this car seat!'

Becoming a mother taught me some pretty rude truths extremely quickly – one of which was that I handle exhaustion about as reasonably as that pantless tiny tyrant in my kitchen from way back when. When I had Olive, my first baby, sleep was no longer on the menu, and I learnt that my brain reacts to being exhausted about as well as Republicans deal with science. There is an enormous divide between actual reality and what we'll call 'Tired Brain Reality', in which I have no idea what the actual fuck is going on around me.

My Tired Brain has made me look like a dead-set dickhead countless times. From the time I planned to quit a god-awful cafe job in spectacular fashion, only to ugly-cry in front of everyone, to the time I planned an inspiring literature class and ended up explaining in great detail what my kids look like when they vomit. Like, I found myself actually acting it out to a room of horrified teenagers. To this day, I have no idea how I kept my teaching registration for as long as I did.

I DIGRESS!

I have never known exhaustion so intimately as when Olive was born. While she is a delightful kid now – kind, considerate, empathetic, helpful and the most mature person in our house – she was a real arsehole of a newborn. She cried endlessly, never smiled or said thank you, would only sleep if I was walking her, and didn't let me sleep for what seemed like forever. I felt like a shell of a person trawling through the streets looking like someone coughed me up. She was underweight, and I couldn't work out why – all I seemed to do was feed and walk her, often at the same time. I had fashioned the BabyBjörn carrier so her face was at tit height, and she would drink as I pounded the pavement. Turns out there wasn't much milk in either tit; she was just starving and using me as a human dummy. If humanity lives much longer, I hope female tits evolve to become transparent so struggling mums out there can see if there's actually milk in their cans or just dust.

On one of my many, many aimless walks around Brunswick with a tiny screaming baby strapped to my chest, I noticed that I was so tired

I felt physically sick. My body ached, my dry eyes stung and everything sounded like I was under water. I could hear my heart beating, and my breathing became shallow, even though, thanks to the endless walking, I was as fit as a mallee bull. The streets were always noisier when she was crying this hard. The lights were always too bright, and it felt like slow and cumbersome people were getting in my way on purpose, like slack-jawed cows.

I was unravelling on Sydney Road, a feeling that became overly familiar as sleep became a distant memory. I looked as good as I felt, too. In inner-city Melbourne, it was hard to tell whether I was a new mum or a hipster who just finished sixteen hours of drinking at a bar lock-in and had found a baby on the way out.

As I walked, I started to notice pain in parts of my body that I didn't even know the names of. What the hell is the part between your shoulder and your elbow called? I know the bit between your elbow and wrist is a forearm, but what is the upper bit? Is it just an arm? How has no one fixed this, and why did mine hurt? From exhaustion? How?!

The physical discomfort, teamed with the search for answers to questions absolutely no one had asked, weighed heavily on me. My baby screamed, my skin throbbed and my brain spun, and soon all of this set me on a path to sheer fury. I stormed down Sydney Road, wondering why the hell no one had thought to warn me how bloody exhausting this was going to be. I felt like a teenager who'd just found out that the cool girls had lied to her about boys liking girls who'd shaved off their eyebrows.

During my pregnancy, unsolicited advice was thrown at me daily. On one occasion, soon after I had announced to my boss I was pregnant, I was at a boring work afternoon tea, and an older male colleague, who I had never had a conversation with, found me and explained that when the baby gets constipated – 'and she will' – I needed to insert parsley into her anus. I was three months pregnant. I hadn't even thought about her anus, let alone her digestive issues, and now I was thinking about foraging for herbs to shove up her bum. Thanks for the tip, mate.

When I was halfway through my pregnancy, I was in the supermarket in the canned tomato section and a lady stopped me and said, 'Make sure your husband is ready for childbirth. It's hard on them too.' I stood there stunned and speechless and, even as I write this, I am overcome with hatred for her. I hope she choked on her spaghetti Bolognese.

For the full nine months, advice seemed to be thrown at me every damn day. So many tips and words of warning. And yet, on this grey Melbourne morning, as I tore up the pavement towards Princes Park, I couldn't for the life of me remember anyone telling me about the complete and utter lack of sleep I would experience. This realisation made me livid. It seemed to be the only warning I needed. Labour was grim, but it lasted a day. Breastfeeding was tricky, but formula was an option (when I finally learnt that my opaque tits were, in fact, useless to a hungry infant). It was the lack of sleep that crushed me, and the part that seemed so obvious to everyone except me.

I picked up my pace; the fire in my empty belly grew. Why did no one tell me that I wouldn't sleep again? Where was the warning? Where was the advice on how to handle it? As the betrayed voice in my head grew louder, I spotted a heavily pregnant woman waiting for the bus. I stopped in my tracks. *I am going to save her.*

Now, this is where my brain severs all ties with actual reality and succumbs completely to 'Tired Brain Reality'.

The Tired Brain narrative went like this:

I looked like a glowing earth mama with flowing, shiny hair and a white linen dress. I had a sweet cherub sleeping peacefully on my plump bosom showing no signs of stirring. I floated over to the woman, who was silently pleading for my advice. She looked up at me, hungry for my pearls of wisdom, and I took her hand in mine. I said, 'Hello, sister. You're about to embark on the most majestic journey of love and nurturing. Your heart will swell, and you will love that baby more than you've ever loved anything in your life. But remember, you will miss sleep so profoundly that you'll wish you slept more during this part, so go home. Work can wait, but sleep cannot. Go and sleep.' And she squeezed my hand, smiled at my sleeping angel and said, 'Thank you so much. You've changed my life forever.' And I floated away.

However, in ACTUAL reality:

Across four lanes of traffic, I saw a pregnant woman patiently waiting for the bus, minding her own business. Without skipping a beat, I yelled, over the sound of my screaming newborn and the idling cars, 'HEY! THIS IS SO BLOODY HARD! PREGNANCY IS EXHAUSTING, BUT WHEN IT IS OVER, IT IS HELL. YOU SHOULD GO HOME RIGHT NOW AND GO TO SLEEP BECAUSE YOU WILL NEVER EVER GET TO DO IT AGAIN WHEN THAT THING COMES OUT OF YOU!'

And, with wide eyes, she looked around her, looked back at me and said, 'Um ... I'm not pregnant.'

Fuck.

So, to the poor woman I scared half to death while making her feel like shit: I am genuinely sorry.

To the delirious little boy running around my kitchen in circles: pull yourself together, for Christ's sake, this isn't a political debate.

And to the tired shell of a woman I will always remember being: you will survive this but please, for the love of god, keep your advice to yourself.

I PITY THE FOOL

I once watched a lady on a plane take up two seats on account of her gloriously large bottom. It wasn't a big deal – no one was sitting next to her so she wasn't spilling onto anyone – but the looks she received from other passengers could only be described as pity mixed with disgust. When I noticed this, I thought about how horrible it would have been for her to book the ticket, let alone line up at the airport, knowing there would be so many extra steps to get through, all of which would need to be communicated in front of an audience. Yes, she'll need a second seat. Yes, she'll need another seatbelt. No, she won't need a wheelchair, no, not even if it is an extra-large wheelchair. I noticed her when I was boarding – she must have been the first one on. I saw her head hung low, avoiding all the judgemental looks. I was struck hard by the knowledge that it was the women who were staring the longest. The men would glance down at her and then quickly look away, and the women would look at her hungrily, as if trying to work out a riddle. How did she get to that size when we were told from childhood to take up less space? It's a cruel reality that women have less patience for another woman's perceived flaws.

I think it boils down to the fact that we expect more from women than from men. Perhaps it's because, for a lot of us, women were more involved in our upbringing, with men more likely to be on the periphery. I remember being in primary school and going to my friends' houses and looking at their stock-standard family photos – you know, the ones where your mum shoves you into the fanciest clothes you own, brushes your hair so hard that you could swear your scalp is bleeding, and drives you to the shopping centre, seething about how she has the worst clothes in the family, and then you get there and you all have to sit way too close to each other, some of you with clasped hands on your lap, others with a hand begrudgingly on a sibling's shoulder, and you're arranged so you look like a human pyramid but a way less fun one, and your mum orders the bulk pack, which includes all different sizes so she can send them to distant relatives as proof that she has single-handedly kept this many children alive for however old the oldest kid is, before finally driving you all home, screaming, *'I just wanted ONE nice photo of us as a family, was THAT SO MUCH TO ASK?!'* You know those ones? Well, I would look at my friends' versions and notice the dad was always at the top of their pyramid and I would think two things:

1) Why does he get to be at the top of the pile?
2) I have never, ever seen that man in my life.

Even in the 'unbroken' families, the dads seemed to be largely absent; still, it was not the men that the mums would whisper about, not even the super-useless ones. I remember when I was seven years old, one friend's mum asked me if my mum was 'okay raising so many kids by herself'. I was confused by this question because I didn't know anything different, so I assumed she was asking me if my mum was sick. I said, 'She's fine.' And the woman tilted her head, wobbling her bouffant perm, and said,

'You poor little thing.' This only confused me more, but I knew I didn't like what was happening. She was pitying me for some reason, and I hated it. I took it as an opportunity to ask for another biscuit, because at seven years old, biscuits taste better than pride.

My mum was judged fiercely by other parents. The other mums loved to pity her and the dads loved to help, and by 'help', I mean hit on her. One dad even jogged past our house at 5am when she would just be getting home from nightshift. He'd pop in for a cuppa in the hope she'd offer him more than milk and sugar. She knew what he was doing, but would have been publicly crucified if she called him out on it, so she just had to smile and hope he didn't actually touch her. I remember those dads very well, and even though I was very young, somewhere deep inside I knew what they were doing. People often think kids are as dumb as a box of hammers, but we learn from every movie that's ever been made that men are always ready to have sex with anything and women should be grateful for the attention but *never* give in to it. Go Grease Lightning!

Mum worked night shifts at a nursing home and we four kids would sleep either in the Tarago in the car park, in the tea room or at home without her. I can't remember sleeping in the car, and I'm grateful for that lapse in memory because it sounds truly terrifying. But I don't feel sorry for myself back then because I know Mum did what she had to do to survive, and also, I was surrounded by my three siblings, who were very loud reminders that I wasn't ever really alone, even when I desperately wanted to be. Also, if I'm completely honest, I love that we went through that pov stage: it makes rich people feel queasy when I bring it up in conversation. I spoke about this chapter of my life in one of my first comedy shows because, while there wasn't much money floating about, there was ample comedic material. We were truly happy, and when I mentioned this on stage, a reviewer, who had decided he hated me before I'd uttered a word, wrote in his scathing review, 'For someone who complained a lot about being poor as a child, it was ironic she decided to make fun of homeless people.' To be clear, I never made fun of homeless people (what kind of monster would do that?) and I was livid about this inaccurate critique, but I was more furious that he'd mistaken my musings about growing up skint as shit as a cry for help or, worse, an invitation to feel sorry for me. The fact that he willingly scrambled my hilarious anecdotes (and yes, they were hilarious – watch 'Probably' on YouTube as proof) into tales of hapless drivel made me want to burn the city to the ground. Growing up poor is never, ever shameful, it's an experience that money literally cannot buy and I wouldn't swap it for all the pork crackling in the world.

But I digress ...

I grew up in the 90s, the decade when gender roles were still very much entrenched in society, and if a woman left her husband she had to fend for herself. Like a lot of absent dads, mine didn't pay child support and Centrelink didn't exist yet, so we got by on the shitty pay she received from working at a nursing home. Mum's work was extremely depressing and most of the oldies in there had one visitor a week at best. Some of the poor things had none. I feel for them now, but as a kid I found them terrifying because they would relish the sight of youth and physically squeeze your small body. One old lady thought she was the Queen of England, and another could only say the word 'two' (although she might have also been saying 'to' and 'too' – hard to say). The most confronting thing about that for me as a five-year-old was that she had no idea the word 'two'/'to'/'too' was coming out; she spoke as if she was telling the most riveting story, and all I wanted to do was cry. It's interesting to me now that I don't remember any of the old blokes on that ward, which might be because I tend to find women more interesting, but I dare say it was because it was more fascinating for me, as a child brought up by formidable women, to see a woman lose her marbles.

I wish I could say I was different from the norm – that I celebrated all women all the time – but I am guilty of holding women to a higher standard. When I had my babies, I was so disappointed in myself for not getting it right straight away (or ever) that I let self-hate envelop me. I found the mums at mothers' group so easy to judge and their husbands so easy to praise. 'Wow, he does one bottle during the night? What a hero! He deserves a weekend away with the boys!' 'Oh, she's having another coffee? Guess she doesn't mind what goes into her breastmilk.'

This harsh gendered lens has stayed with me through comedy, unfortunately. I'm in a male-dominated industry and, more often than not, line-ups reflect this. It would make sense to me that I would champion any female comedian I ever saw, but I find myself to be subconsciously quite harsh on them. Don't get me wrong, I gravitate towards funny women. But even though I find women funnier (has Judith Lucy ever not been the funniest comedian on the bill?) and I will binge whatever series UK comedic genius Daisy May Cooper stars in, I still find myself putting more pressure on women than I do men. Year after year at the Melbourne Comedy Festival, the formidable Urzila Carlson effortlessly wins the People's Choice Award (most tickets sold), and Kitty Flanagan often comes second. We live in a time when women often sell more tickets than men, which is thrilling. But the lengths we have to go to to be taken seriously in this industry are mind-blowing. So if I am in a line-up with all men and one other woman, I will watch that woman super critically: if she isn't better than the men, or at least as good as them, I worry that we will have missed an opportunity to show that women are worthy of taking up space in comedy.

Is this fair? Hell, no. Do I feel good about admitting this? Fuck, no. But unfortunately it's how women have been programmed to view each other: unforgivingly.

One of my greatest shames in my career was slagging off a female comedian to a bunch of other comedians in a car. I was tired and she had genuinely annoyed me, and I basically blacked out and let the vile nastiness spew out of my face and into the Mazda SUV, to wash over three shocked people I barely knew. At the time, I thought they were nodding along with me, but they weren't. They were just letting me show the worst side of myself until I ran out of steam. The next day, I apologised to them because it wasn't only unprofessional, it was truly embarrassing for me to have been such a bitch. I thought my humble apology would be the end of it – I would learn a valuable lesson to never again be such a moll about a colleague to other colleagues, and they would decide that I wasn't a heartless monster and that I'd embarrassed myself enough to let it go. Unfortunately, it didn't work out that way. One of them thought it was important that the subject of my beef know what I had said, which was so unnecessary. I felt betrayed by her lack of 'girl code', but mostly I just felt awful that I had thrown another woman under the bus for fodder.

As soon as I found out she was aware of the bitchy shit I'd said, I called her and apologised, and she was so lovely about it. In fact she said, 'We've all been mean before, let's move on.' And she was right, we *have* all been mean, but it's rare we hear the awful things other people say about us. I still feel a lot of shame about what I said and I will never forget how easy it was for me to turn into a nasty moll given the opportunity. I'm not making excuses for it – everything I said was regrettably mean-spirited and 100 per cent optional – but it did remind me that I am a product of my social upbringing. I became one of my friends' mums who'd bitched about my mum and pretended they had a good reason.

We women have a complicated relationship with each other and, while I offer no solution, I do suggest a moment to consider why we do it. I reckon it's because we've been taught to keep each other lower than the blokes who consistently disappoint but are nailing it if they show up for one bottle-feed or a family photo. And we women owe each other more.

To the large lady on the plane, and the women tut-tutting her for getting so big; to the woman who lost her words but not her stories and the mums who had to let their kids sleep in the tearoom; to the women who fucked up enough to blame other women for their sour mood or shitty husband – we all have so much to unlearn. We owe that to the little girls watching us tear each other down – they don't see it as us being strong, they see it as the reason we're seen as small to begin with.

BREAST IS BEST (OR SOME SHIT)

'You're going to have to come in and weigh her in two days.' The maternal health care nurse was a salt-of-the-earth type woman in her fifties with silvery eyeshadow, strong shoulders and an impressive bosom. She had the voice of someone who'd smoked for decades and box-dyed mahogany hair that glistened under the harsh fluorescent lights of the council-run clinic. She drove a purple metallic Holden Commodore to home visits, and to this day I think it is the loudest car I have ever heard. I loved her. She had worked as a maternal health care nurse for about 450 years and she didn't bother with any of the posh new ways to raise a baby. She was very clear that she thought all the new fads were utter bullshit, which was music to my ears. One of her catchphrases was 'A baby is a baby. Always has been, always will be.' I. Loved. Her.

'Two days?' I asked, pulling a singlet over Olive's head. She was four months old by this stage, or 2920 hours old, depending on how you measure a baby's life. I prefer the latter because the number 'four' seems so insignificant. I think I've gone four months with something in my teeth before anyone has pointed it out. Four months? Who cares?

But 2920 hours? That feels serious. I cannot think of *anything* I would want to do for 2920 hours.

- Let's recap: 2920 hours of being a mother. Of that:
- 2590 hours were spent listening to Olive scream.
- 2000 hours were spent walking her up and down cobblestone alleys.
- 900 hours were spent calling my sister Amy, asking her what the fuck I was doing wrong.
- 850 hours were spent listening to Amy telling me that I was doing everything right, but 'some babies are just harder than others and Olive is a mongrel'.
- 10 hours were spent asleep.
- 2919 hours were spent breastfeeding.

I fed her CONSTANTLY. We co-slept and she fed all night long. I'd fashioned the baby carrier so she could feed as we walked through the freezing Melbourne winter. I fed her at cafes, barbecues, parks, funerals, weddings and even on the toilet. I fed her even when I was made to feel totally uncomfortable about it.

When Olive was one month old, or 730 hours old, depending on how you measure clusterfeeding, we took her to a pub on Sydney Road to celebrate our friend's birthday. I'd dyed my hair and put on makeup for the first time since she was born, applying more concealer to the bags under my eyes than ever before. I stuffed myself into my skinny jeans with rips in the knees, as was the fashion in 2014, sucking in my soft stomach as I buttoned them up. I was beyond proud of myself for fitting back into them already and put it down to being a young mum, but really it was because I'd walked about a million miles since Olive was born because listening to her cry outdoors was slightly less awful than listening to her cry in our apartment.

I was the first of these friends to have a baby, so Olive was a little foreign concept brought to life and made to sit on my lap on a ripped corduroy armchair in a dingy Brunswick pub. I'd fed her for hours and hours and hours before we got there in the hope that she would sleep for the duration of our stay and everyone would fawn over her and praise me for having such a perfect bebe. But she didn't do that. Almost immediately she wailed as if I had pinched her and, hot with shame, I pulled my singlet down and slipped a boob in her mouth. I'd spent most of the last 730 hours like this, so the novelty of breastfeeding had worn off and I was taken aback to hear a friend's sister say, 'Oh my god!' and then physically turn her body away from me as if I had just shat on the retro tiled coffee table. I frantically pretended I was comfortable and looked down to watch Olive feed to avoid seeing any more of my friends recoil at the sight of me.

When she was finished feeding (she never was, lol), I gave her to Lukasz and went to the bar to get myself a light beer. As I patiently stood there, acknowledging how wonderfully empty my arms felt, I heard the lady in front of me making a complaint to the bartender about 'a woman breastfeeding in front of everyone'. My face flushed red and I wanted to leave, but my feet remained fused to the floor. The bartender nodded and said to the woman, 'Look, we can't ask her to leave, but she really should have a blanket over her.'

A blanket. Over Olive's head? In summer? I turned on my heels and went back to Lukasz. 'We have to go,' I said, red-faced, as I gathered all of our things into the gigantic nappy bag. 'Someone is complaining about me.'

He tried to talk me out of it, telling me not to worry what those dumb bitches thought, but the damage was done. I needed to go home to our miniature one-bedroom apartment and remind myself that things like the pub weren't for me anymore. My pub days were over. I may have only been twenty-seven years old, but a chapter had ended before I even knew it and it stung. I was a mum now and, for a lot of people, mums were too confronting to look at in spaces they didn't belong.

That shame was chipped away over the next three months, or 2190 hours, depending on how you measure your shame. Olive's relentless crying was much worse than any judgement of idiots, so I fed her everywhere. I honestly couldn't have fed her more if I'd tried.

So when I went in to weigh her and she was medically underweight, my eyes stung as I held back tears. How? How could this baby, who had spent the last four months literally sucking the life out of me, be underweight? The only person who spent more time eating was Brad Pitt in every movie he has ever been in.

I picked Olive up and shoved her on my boob and she sucked and sucked and sucked. She looked at me and I knew I looked like shit. My hair had about two inches of mousy brown regrowth and was in dire need of a trim. My skin was grey with exhaustion and my clothes were stained and dishevelled. I couldn't remember the last time I'd put effort into the way I looked because everything to do with me at this point in my life seemed entirely trivial, like putting mascara on a pig.

'How much weight could she put on in two days?' I asked, trying to control the wobble in my voice. The nurse quickly looked away from me in case I did start crying. She would have hated that just as much as I would. To cry in front of a powerhouse like her would have been mortifying. Women like her don't like weakness; they see it as a waste of time, like decorating cupcakes or sending Christmas cards.

'It's more to see if she loses any,' she said. 'Because if she loses weight, we have to rethink our strategy.'

'Strategy?' I thought. 'Did we make a strategy? Did I zone out of that strategy meeting?' It definitely sounded like the kind of meeting I would have zoned out of.

'Right,' I said slowly. 'What strategy are we doing now?'

'Breastfeeding, Bron. You're breastfeeding her.' Her brow furrowed as she searched my face. I realised she thought I was insane.

'Oh, yeah, I know I'm breastfeeding her,' I scoffed, slightly embarrassed. 'I'm doing that *all the bloody time*.' I looked down at Olive and back at the nurse. 'How the hell could she lose weight when all she does is feed?' I was flabbergasted.

'Well, we don't know how much milk is actually coming out. Maybe there isn't much in there for her at all.'

Oh. I'd never considered that. I just thought if she was sucking, then she was drinking, and if she was drinking, then she would be growing, and if she was growing then I was doing my job. But she wasn't growing, which meant she wasn't drinking, which meant there wasn't enough milk and I was not doing my job. I was not feeding my child. Fuck.

Again, I found myself fighting back tears because it all seemed so fucking obvious all of a sudden.

'And what do we do if she loses weight?' I asked.

The nurse sighed. 'What are your views on formula?'

'Views? I have no views on formula. It actually looks amazing. Am I allowed to, you know, just give that to her?' Even as the words came out of my mouth, I knew how fucking ridiculous they were. Women in my mothers' group gave their babies formula all the time, but I thought that if you *could* breastfeed, you had to. It just goes to show, exhaustion can turn you into a first-class idiot.

'Allowed to?' She laughed. 'You can give that baby formula all the bloody time! If you have nothing against the stuff and, trust me, the stuff is miraculous, you should go get it. Lord knows it'll help her sleep.'

The harsh fluorescent lights warmed as she said this. The icy edge in the room seemed to dissipate and I had a sudden urge to hug her. 'It'll help her sleep?'

'Oh, Christ, yeah! It'll fill her belly like cement and she'll be out of it like a drunk bloke on the piss.' Her relief at my openness to formula was palpable.

I thought about all the extra visits to the clinic I had been making, at her request, and it dawned on me that this was what she'd wanted to begin with. 'Why didn't you tell me about this earlier?' I asked.

'Oh, well, you new mothers are crazy about breastfeeding. The shit you new mums go through to avoid formula must be bloody exhausting. I just didn't want to offend you.'

Offend me? A wave of frustration hit me as I thought about all the unnecessary crying I'd endured from my baby who was technically starving. I'd walked countless kilometres with her either screaming or sucking at my body and for what? Because the nurse didn't want to offend me? Frankly, I was offended.

I got up and put Olive into the baby carrier, shoving my boob back into her mouth. I shook the frustration off and focused on the new strategy, which was replacing the old strategy I didn't remember putting in place. 'I'll be back in two days and we can weigh her then. She will definitely have put on weight! Mark my words.' I was elated. Finally, someone had a potential answer to why Olive was so miserable! Yes, it was my fault, but I was also going to fix it! Hooray!

I charged out of the clinic into the freezing late afternoon. The sun was going down, and even though I knew it would be dark by the time I walked to Coles, I powered on. In retrospect it would have been way faster for me to walk home and get the car – home was closer to the clinic than Coles, but reason and logic paled next to the idea of an easier life with Olive. I felt empowered, and the only way I could physically walk was towards the formula aisle.

I stormed down the aisle and called Amy. 'Which formula should I get?'

'Formula? Oh, good for you! This is a great idea. She's going to sleep like a log!'

What? How did she know this as well? Amy had breastfed all four of her babies until the next baby was born and bumped them off the tit trough, which is exactly what our mum did with her billions of kids. Why hadn't Amy told me about this secret to sleeping? Was it a secret everyone knew? I decided not to question her, I was too distracted by the zillions of bright coloured formula tins in front of me. Why were there so many of them? Did they all do the same thing? I looked at the price tag: $31? Holy hell! How do the poor mums with useless tits feed their babies?

Amy suggested one her friend used with her baby, and that was all I needed to hear. I picked it up and practically ran to the checkout.

My freedom was in my hands – the end of the hard part was in sight! I couldn't contain my excitement. I beamed at the apathetic checkout girl who would have been about sixteen years old. 'This is her first formula tin. She's never had it before!'

The girl looked blankly at me. I may as well have been saying, 'I had a dream last night and my friend Nikki was in it, but she wasn't Nikki, she had an accent but in the dream it seemed normal for her to have an accent ...' I guess what I'm saying here is people care just as much about what milk your baby drinks as they do about your boring-as-fuck dreams. Just get on with it.

I called Mum on the walk home in the dark and told her about the new strategy, which was essentially just feeding my baby. I should have known better because she replied, 'Oh, thank god. I've been so worried about that baby. She's so skinny and so, so, so hungry, Bronnie.' Misstep, Hels. She was trying to be supportive, and I appreciate it's hard to know what to say to a new mum drowning in uncertainty, but that was entirely incorrect. How long had she worried about her weight? Had Amy worried about her weight and not said anything? Had they spoken to each other about me starving my baby? Had everyone known that Olive was desperate for formula except me?

Why the fuck were there so many secrets in motherhood? Who was the gatekeeper of them, and why were they drip-fed to us slowly, and often after we'd already made a million mistakes? Early motherhood has got to be the loneliest time of a woman's life, and the secrecy around it amplifies the feeling that you truly are working all of this out by yourself.

I felt betrayed and stupid, but I pushed all that down and focused on the silver lining: for the first time in maybe her whole life, my daughter will be full and we will all sleep.

By the time I got home I couldn't feel my hands as I clumsily and excitedly warmed up her dinner of mashed pumpkin. I popped Olive in her highchair to feed her the orange sludge she would inevitably spit out, and then scooped her up and ran her bath, all the while humming and singing like a madwoman. I was ecstatic: for the first time in 2920 hours, I was going to sleep for longer than two hours at a time! Heaven was only a few hours away!

I dried her off, put her pyjamas on her wriggly, clean, pink body and kissed her soft cheeks over and over and over. Sleep was on the horizon for her and me. The key was in that bright yellow tin on the kitchen bench!

I gently pushed her clean, pink legs into her Bonds onesie taking a moment to look at how skinny they were. I zipped her up and carried her downstairs where I could start the fattening-up process. I prepared the bottle and tasted it. It tasted like Clag, but it promised something glorious, so I shoved the bottle in her mouth and she gulped it down, wide-eyed. It spilled out of the corners of her mouth and pooled on the space between her lovely bald head and my arm. She was loving it! She was going to sleep! We were both going to sleep! I didn't believe in marriage, but I was starting to think I could marry baby formula! Everything was going to be okay!

To my surprise, the elation started to fade and a pang of sadness hit me deep in my guts.

Sadness not only because the one motherhood skill I thought I had was coming to an end. Sadness not only because the closeness of feeding her with the body that had created her was being replaced with something literally anyone could do for her. But sadness, mostly, that I had let my baby be hungry for so long.

For 2920 hours to be exact.

The guilt I felt for failing Olive didn't ease for ages. I'm not sure it even has, twelve years later, or 105,192 hours later, depending on how you measure your guilt.

Motherhood is laden with guilt even when you're getting it right, which often feels incredibly rare. If I could go back to that moment of feeding her with formula for the first time, I would say to myself two things:

1. Your tits are going to thank you for this.
2. While you're never going to forget any of this, she won't remember a thing.

Olive slept that night and only woke twice, which was transformative for our little family. Olive and I had more sleep than we'd had since I became her mother and it felt like a layer of clay was cracking on my skin and I was re-emerging as something new. I beamed as I told Lukasz he could now help with night feeds, and he was genuinely relieved. I guess it would be awful to watch someone you love fade under the weight of a responsibility they can't share.

When I went back to the maternal health care nurse two days later I wore my skinny jeans with rips in the knees and the colour had returned to my face. I'd racked up more sleep over the past two nights than I had in the past month and I felt like a million bucks. The nurse smiled at me as she weighed Olive and we both clapped when we saw the number. I bloody did it! Well, formula did it – my baby girl had put on weight!

The nurse smiled at me and said, 'Well done, Mum. You're doing a great job.'

I didn't say anything in reply because I knew if I did I would risk flooding the clinic with a million heavy tears. I just sat there and let myself feel the fleeting sense of pride that only appears every so often in early motherhood. I didn't let myself cry in front of her because I knew that strong women hate when other women cry, and I owed this magical woman at least the gift of stoicism.

Just before I closed the door behind me, I heard her pluck a tissue from the box and gently say, 'You can cry now. Everything is going to be just fine.' And I still don't know if she was talking to me or to herself.

ALL ABOARD THE SLEEP TRAIN(ING)

I'd read somewhere that sleep deprivation was a form of torture, and when I was exhausted with a newborn I never believed anything more in my life. Well, maybe it was a tie with Cillian Murphy being the hottest man in the world, but both can be equally true. Cillian, if you're reading this (and why wouldn't you – the star of *Peaky Blinders* and owner of the most gorgeous blue eyes and bone structure on the planet – be reading a book about an Australian woman's experience of losing her mind after having children? You're the perfect man, feminist and ally!) then please know that I am free to hang out whenever you are. I am less mental now and I reckon we could be best friends with a palpable undercurrent of sexual tension that we never act on. Hit me up on Instagram, or just show up at my house, I'm flexible.

Anyway, Olive didn't sleep much at all, probably because she was literally starving #LOL. From birth I fed her to sleep (well, that's what I thought I was doing) or walked powerfully up and down cobblestone alleys until she knocked herself out. By the time she was four months old, or 2920 hours old, I could count on one hand how many times she had drifted off to sleep in her cot. I could also have counted on one hand how many times she'd done it if I'd been a double amputee because she had NEVER done it. Zero times. She slept all night on my boob – I just lay on my side and she used me as a human milk bar, which was slightly confronting after we learnt my boobs were pretty much ornamental. She didn't take a dummy, so I stepped up to the plate and became the biggest, most exhausted dummy on the planet. I really should put that on my LinkedIn profile.

For the first few months of Olive's life, it was manageable. I was twenty-seven, so my body could withstand extreme discomfort and very little sleep for longer than it could now, but everyone has a limit on torture. Around month four, none of our sleep hacks were working for us anymore and we were splitting at the seams. She couldn't be fed to sleep because she would finish her milk faster, and she was getting too big for us to rock her to sleep.

I'd only just solved the mystery of the starvation (the cure was food #ROFL), but I had not solved the mystery of sleep, so the screaming continued. Sure, the sleeping had improved once she wasn't starving anymore, but she had returned to waking at least four times a night, and we found ourselves at our wits' end. Again.

Each night I would scroll the internet searching for the answer, and every site reiterated that everything that I had done so far was INCORRECT. Good. No, seriously, that's actually great. I should never have walked her to sleep, I should never have co-slept and I should never, ever, ever have fed her to sleep. Every single way Olive had drifted off had been a huge no-no and now I had broken her. The nights were bloody long, so I had so many extra hours to search the internet for a solution. Time and time again, sponsored ads popped up for instructional manuals to help your baby sleep, and I was ready to buy all of them. The blurbs of these books all seemed to say the same thing: my baby wasn't sleeping because I had made too many mistakes in the early stages of her life. I learnt that even my instincts for Olive were wrong, which stung my tired heart. I'd thought my newborn baby needed the closeness of her mother, to hold her, feed her, let her lie on me for as long as she wanted, but apparently this assumption was not only wrong, but also apparently damaging for her. Fucking fuck.

The more I read, the more I came to believe I had committed a terrible crime and now both of us would have to face severe consequences. The internet told me that I had coddled her for my own selfish reasons and the road out of this mess was long, gruelling and unavoidable. The internet weighed up my reprehensible actions and decided upon a punishment to fit my crime: sleep training.

Sleep training, basically, is putting your tiny baby in their cot, leaving the room and letting them scream until they give up and go to sleep. I desperately didn't want to do it. It meant enduring torture fit for the worst scum on earth, like Ivan Milat or Peter Dutton, and I was beyond terrified.

I read guidebook after guidebook on sleep training before I started, and each one filled me with a combination of hope, dread and guilt (wow, it's almost like everything in motherhood elicits guilt #LMAO). All of these ~~manifestos~~ guidebooks had slightly different strategies, but essentially they were the same: let them cry a lot.

Now, I don't know the exact science behind memories and why we keep certain ones and forget others, but I know we remember moments that come with heightened emotions. Like the first day of school, or seeing your baby for the first time, or the first time you get yelled at by a friend's mum, or a kiss that stops time. We remember the things that push us to truly feel something for the first time, kind of like a checking point in your wiring to let you know you've hit a new level of emotion.

The best example I have for this is when I was eleven and felt maternal guilt for the first time. You would be correct in your mathematical findings that I wasn't even a real mother at that age. I vividly remember going on the Wipeout ride at Dreamworld with my My Baby toy clipped onto the zip of my Piping Hot jacket. Remember My Baby toys? They were the 'girl' answer to Tamagotchis – you had to keep a human baby alive instead of an alien creature. How dare we girls ever think that we could nurture something other than a human baby, even if it was a pretend one? Little girls are trained for the responsibility of motherhood from birth, yet we still feel wildly unqualified when it happens. Maybe we should just cut to the chase and give little girls baby dolls that cry, praise them when they look a certain way and tell them their body isn't actually theirs. Oh wait, we already do that. Sorry, baby mamas! (If you think the gendered toys are entirely innocent, just look at the toys we give little boys: cars and guns, things that make them feel powerful and in control. Pretty cool stuff #IMO.)

This memory at Dreamworld will stick with me forever because I was terrified that as the ride flipped and turned, the My Baby toy would unclip from my zipper and fall into the shallow water below, where a mechanical shark with chipped paint and missing teeth circled menacingly. I remember this so clearly because it was maybe the most petrified I had ever been – something that I had devoted countless hours to keeping safe was in danger, and it would have been entirely my fault if she died. I did not scream once on that ride – I was frozen with fear – and when the ride slowed to a stop, my relief was replaced quickly with self-chastising, for being so careless with her. For the rest of the day, I held on to the My Baby toy tightly, never truly shaking the feeling that I'd almost lost her forever.

I know I remember this because of the extreme emotion it elicited, so it makes sense that our brains are branded with the memories that ultimately change us. I wish I could say that this initial instance of maternal guilt was the worst it ever got, but when sleep training began, I realised it could mutate and grow into a beast that would almost destroy me.

The ~~manifestos~~ guidebooks said to keep a diary. I wrote down what time she woke up for the day, what time she ate, drank milk and then what time I put her back down. She was 2920 hours old and counting, so her 'awake windows' were only ninety minutes long, during which all the feeding, cuddling and daily chores needed to be done before the dreadful sleep training began again.

Putting Olive down was extraordinarily difficult. My arms would tense up as I lowered her warm little body into the big, cold cot, which had been used as an installation piece since we'd moved into the townhouse. I remember when we put the cot together, I took a photo of her inside it to share with family group chats and then, as quick as a flash, scooped her back up into my arms. It felt right, her being so close to me, so when she became too big to rock, and my milk was running so low that I couldn't feed her to sleep anymore, sleep training was presenting itself as simultaneously the only and the worst solution.

Once she was in the cot, I would sit with her for ten minutes, patting her and singing 'Incy Wincy Spider' over and over and over. A lot of the guidebooks said that staying in the room only prolonged the desired result – the baby learning how to self-soothe – but I physically couldn't leave her in there by herself. I had to work my way up to that, and it took every bit of strength I had.

When I did leave, I would scurry down the stairs, listening to her screaming, and flick on the kettle. I had read that if you stand near a kettle, the sound of the water warming up distracts you and, by the time it has boiled, the baby might be asleep. That never happened. Olive would scream and scream and I would stare at the clock on the wall until I was 'allowed' to go back in. The guidebooks said to leave her for at least ten minutes, and they were the longest ten minutes of my life. I dread to think what she was thinking as she thrashed about in her cot, all alone, with hot tears streaming down her face.

After the ten minutes I was 'allowed' to go back in and pat her again. If she was really beside herself, which of course she always was, I was 'allowed' to pick her up, give her a cuddle until her twitching body calmed down, and then reluctantly place her back in her cot, which was now damp with her tears, and start the ten minutes over again. I'd empty the kettle, fill it to the brim and flick it on. I would put my ear next to the loudest part of the appliance and rest my cheek on the cold marble bench, hoping that *this time* would be the time she 'worked it out'.

Eventually she would get to sleep – not because she had 'worked it out', but because she was too tired to keep crying. She would literally cry herself to sleep, and I would spend her nap once again staring at the clock, nerves completely fried, wondering how many sleep cycles she would get through before the ninety-minute awake window would start again.

This 'training' went on for weeks, with next to no progress. I rarely left the house because I wanted to give her my undivided attention when she was awake to show her how much I loved her and how sorry I was that I had stuffed her sleep so badly to begin with. When I had to go to the shops, I walked down Sydney Road with her strapped to the front of me in the baby carrier. I loved feeling her so close to me, even when she was upset; I needed her on me, to feel like I was at least there for her, like a useless sack of bones. I walked past bars, cafes and shops with smiling people in them who were leading normal lives and I wondered what I looked like to them. Catching a glimpse of myself in a shop window, I gasped. I looked like I had been dragged along the road by wild horses and then dumped at a Salvation Army to dress myself. My leggings were pilling and my grey cardigan had pumpkin soup slopped down the front of it. I didn't recognise the woman with the sunken eyes and limp shoulders. What had I become?

I found myself walking into a bookshop and searching for a book that didn't exist. I wanted to read a book about what I was going through, but with answers to all my questions. I needed it to tell me exactly what to do next, how long this hell would last and that we would emerge relatively unscathed. I found a book about a struggling mother with a seemingly tear-smudged font on the cover. I figured that this was as close to what I was after as I could find, and I went to the counter to buy it. The woman who worked there wore an emerald green apron. She took the book from my hands and looked directly at me. Knowing exactly how I looked, I didn't look back at her.

'Are you ... are you okay?' she asked.

I looked up at her. Her face looked so worried, and I had a strange urge to be hugged by her. 'Me? Yeah, I'm fine. We're sleep training.' I smiled weakly. 'It's killing me.'

'Oh,' she said sympathetically. 'I remember doing that with my daughter. It gets better. You just have to get through this bit.'

I thanked her for her words of encouragement, but I was disappointed that this learned older mother didn't give me permission to just stop and hold Olive forever.

I walked home in the freezing air, making sure Olive was still awake. A step backwards in this hellscape would have been absolutely brutal, so I tickled her little feet and sang the alphabet loudly the whole way home, with a book under my arm that would hopefully fix this whole mess.

I wish I could say it quickly became easier, but it didn't. The tear-smudged book did not fix anything. It was unrelatable and harrowing and made me feel even more hopeless than before. It promoted the idea that motherhood is the loneliest time in a woman's life, and when we share our experiences with each other, we run the risk of feeling even more isolated.

In this mindset, even when Olive finally started to sleep, my strung-out brain told me she had grown accustomed to me abandoning her, so there was no real plus side for ages. She still woke many times in a night, and I still sang 'Incy Wincy Spider' a million times a day, so the torture lasted long enough to irreparably damage my nervous system. I cringe at the thought of what it did to hers.

They say sleep deprivation is torture, but in hindsight, sleep training my innocent, bewildered baby was much, much worse. The training was brutal, and I did it with all three of my babies. I didn't do it because I'd decided I'd broken one, so I may as well break the others. I did it because it was the only way I knew how to do it. For Edie and Ari, I hired qualified nurses to come sit with me and help me through it, but it was still horrific. If I could go back in time, I don't know if I'd do sleep training again. It did help my babies sleep and as as far as I can tell they're unharmed by it, but I will forever remember that time with insurmountable pangs of guilt, like the bringing My Baby toy to Dreamworld, but probably worse. As I write this chapter, I posed the same question to Lukasz. 'Of course I would do it again. How elese would they learn how to self settle?' He looked at me curiously, then rubbed my back. 'But it was different for me,' he said. 'You're the mum. I imagine it was harder for you.' And he, like he so often is, was right.

All of which is to say: Cillian, if you're still reading this, I threw out that grey stained cardigan and my kids now know how to sleep, so if you want to hang out, I can make time for you. I'll pop the kettle on and rest my face next to it for old times' sake

SAD LADY AT THE PARTY

Entering into motherhood was like a whirlwind, but with less wind and more shit, tears and general chaos. As I've mentioned, within sixteen months of first meeting, Lukasz and I had our first baby. So while I was getting to know my baby, I was also getting to know him and who the hell I was as a mother, and we've already established how much I bloody hate learning.

Throughout my first pregnancy, I struggled to decide on the best time to tell people, and I wasn't really sure why I didn't just blurt it out to everyone. I certainly wasn't ashamed or worried about what people thought about me becoming a mother, and I definitely wanted to *be* a mother, but the whole thing just felt too personal to share. I am not very open about my emotions – not because I'm mysterious or calculated, but because I'm extremely avoidant. One way to avoid hard or complicated feelings is to never talk about them, which is not only a great tip, but an unhealthy one. You're welcome.

I had just started teaching at my dream school and it took me six attempts to tell my principal about being pregnant. I also kept it from my students until it was comically obvious I was pregnant – the buttons on my dress bursting down the front, threatening to pop off and take out the front tooth of one of the students in the first row. Before I was obviously pregnant, there was an awkward stage of *Is she? Isn't she?* One day I overheard a Year 12 girl named Rhiannon hiss at another student, 'So what?! My mum stacks it on when she's stressed and teaching looks stressful, so leave her alone, you idiot.' I felt so warm with pride, almost like I'd just consumed half a litre of hot chocolate. Because I had.

This hesitation about telling people wasn't reserved only for work. I didn't tell my best mate Claire until I was three months pregnant, and I usually kept nothing from her. I finally told her on my birthday, because she was less likely to get upset with me on that day, but I can't ever forget the hurt in her eyes as she showered me with excitement. She didn't say anything, but I could tell she couldn't understand why I had kept such monumental news from her for three whole months, and I couldn't understand it either.

Perhaps it was because my life was evolving into a chapter in which I would feel exposed and vulnerable, and the gravity of this was quite daunting, or maybe it was the last time I could feel like this baby was mine and not everyone else's? Was it possible I didn't want to feel like their reactions mattered to me? Or because I wanted to articulate to myself what this all meant before other people told me what it meant for them? Or was it because I was only twenty-six years old and I knew how much stigma there was about teen pregnancies? (I know twenty-six isn't technically teen years, but compared to the settled and mature mothers around me, I was basically in Year 8.) I still don't know the answer to that, but I do know that sharing my babies has been the greatest gift I have given this world, and one of the hardest things I do each and every day, knowing the world doesn't deserve them.

Olive was born on 9 February 2014, and she was absolutely perfect. Everyone guessed she would be a chubby boy with a thick mop of hair, but she was the skinniest and baldest baby girl in the world. I loved that she proved everyone wrong and, honestly, she's continued to do that every damn day of her life.

Still, perfect or not, we all know that Olive proved to be a really unsettled baby. She only liked the pram when I pushed it up and down cobblestones so she would get thrashed around until she stopped screaming and went to sleep. I know every cobblestone alley in Brunswick and they still give me a complicated mix of emotions when I walk down them.

The cobblestones I spent the most time walking up and down were on Cocoa Jackson Lane, which was next to a plumbers' workshop whose employees would nod at me when they walked in and out, a small offering of recognition that I still existed. I could spend over an hour walking up and down that dank, grey lane. Every single morning, Olive would turn on the waterworks for the water workers. I must have been the chief plumber's nemesis, but at this point in my life I didn't have the capacity to give a shit about that. Come to think of it, none of those plumbers ever asked me if I was okay, but I guess I should be grateful because I dread to think what my response would have been. Probably 'What do you think?! This is fucked! Why does she cry so much?! Help me!' Yeah, best they kept their distance actually.

Every morning on Cocoa Jackson Lane, a beautiful and kind woman named Mez walked past me with a skinny latte in each hand and a soft smile on her lovely face. The smile was for me, but the lattes weren't – they were for her and her daughter, Lauren, who just so happened to be in my mothers' group with a baby two days younger than mine. Lauren lived just off Cocoa Jackson Lane and every morning Mez would walk to her house with love, patience and caffeine. If Lauren hadn't been so excellent I would have been livid that she was lucky enough to have a mum so readily available during the hardest era of her life. I *could* have also been jealous of Lauren's perfectly behaved baby girl, Claudia, who slept through every mothers' group meeting to the point that I was convinced the muslin wrap over the silent pram was hiding an empty bassinet. Claudia slept through the night way faster than Olive did and, if Lauren wasn't so brilliant as a mate, I would have given her the finger as she walked her silent baby away from the cafe. Claudia was like a tiny X-Man – not even Olive's shrill and constant screams woke her. Thankfully, Lauren never seemed to pity or lecture me on where I was going wrong. I will always be grateful for that. I hate to admit it, but if, for my firstborn, I'd had a baby as perfect as Claudia, I would have been so up myself that I would have written a book on parenting within the first few months. The world should be grateful that I got a hard one first, because I was humbled to the point of never offering parenting advice to anyone ever. I think. I can't remember actually. God, I hope I haven't.

It was bittersweet seeing Mez each morning. I was grateful Lauren had a mum there to help, but a small part of me resented her for having a 'shortcut'. I've come to learn that in moments of vulnerability and hardship, it's impossible for me not to compare myself to others who seem to have it easier. In saying that, if my mum had moved into our one-bedroom apartment during those chaotic months, it wouldn't have ended well. Hels made the right decision to give me space during that time, even though I felt sick from loneliness.

Those walks gave me a lot of time to think, and when Olive was sleeping, I would allow myself to dream about easier times ahead. One of my favourite days to fantasise about was Olive's first birthday party. It would be summer, friends and family would be gathered together, she would be toddling around and giggling at bubbles and friends' dogs, there would be cake and champagne, and *no one* would be crying. The image of this perfect day to celebrate her not being a screaming newborn anymore really kept me going. It felt like the biggest milestone I would ever celebrate and, eleven years and two more kids later, getting to the end of the first year of motherhood still feels incomparable. It quickly became my favourite day to think about.

Then Olive's first birthday party arrived and it wasn't just awful, it was the perfect representation of the year I'd just endured. The weather was stunning and, yes, there was both cake and champagne. The colour scheme was orange, green and blue because I had convinced myself these were Olive's favourite colours in a desperate attempt to distance her from gendered norms (kill me). The sun was shining on my friends' bare shoulders and Lukasz's and my families had travelled interstate to be there. My brother Hamish had lent me his gigantic backyard for the celebration and he had helped me hang blue, green and orange decorations on the trees and Hills hoist. There were snacks, and Claire had made a monster-themed cake as a gentle nod to how Olive had acted as a newborn. We had all the ingredients for a perfect day.

Everyone I loved or even liked was there and there were toddlers laughing – but not my toddler. Olive was so overwhelmed by everything that she cried for the entire party. She wasn't sure why people were thrusting presents at her, and she had decided absolutely everyone at the party, except for me, was poisonous. People tried to help – they tried to hold her for me or pass me a drink – but she would cling to me and thrash around so ferociously that she'd smash the drink out of my hand. Dressed in my nan's orange polka-dot party dress, I stood in the middle of my brother's backyard and watched everyone have a nice time and occasionally look at me with pity. It was no different to any of the 365 days that led up to this party that I had wanted so badly. The party to mark the end of a brutal year: The Brutal Party.

That night, after I got Olive to sleep, I sat in my tiny courtyard with Claire and Lukasz and bawled my eyes out. Sure, I felt disappointed that it hadn't been the day I'd yearned for, but mostly I felt immense guilt that I resented Olive for ruining a day she didn't understand. It's always when they go to sleep that they become completely blameless and you let the weight of insurmountable guilt pin you to a chair. I laughed about how silly it was to think Olive would be a happy baby for the day, when she had been so cross for most of her first year. I cried about how I thought I was to blame for her less-than-sunny disposition (if I'm honest, I still feel responsible for her being such a miserable baby). I felt like I had let her down and, as much as I know this isn't true, I felt like she let me down too.

In the warm summer's night, I sipped a glass of rosé and cringed reflecting on the conversations I had had that day hoping I wasn't too dismissive or, god forbid, honest. My filter had completely eroded and I let people see how much I wasn't enjoying my baby's party, which must have been confronting for everyone. There is something stingingly incongruent about a sad, washed-out woman standing among orange, green and blue balloons while Taylor Swift's 'Shake It Off' plays. As I described the hellish day to two of the people who loved me the most, I felt like my skull was cracking open and my skin was too sensitive to touch. I knew I was speaking too quickly and I could feel my feet slipping out from under me. I felt completely unhinged, which took my breath away because, as I sat in my tiny courtyard, it dawned on me that this detachment from reality was something I'd felt before.

Just before I went to bed that night, I went into the bathroom and took a pregnancy test. Two blue lines stared back at me. One for each baby my body had created. I looked at myself in the mirror without breathing, and then Olive began to cry.

I'M IN CHAINS

Everyone remembers exactly where they were and what they were doing for the following three moments in history:

Princess Diana's death.

September 11.

The first time they heard Tina Arena's song 'Chains'.

All three of these things happened during my childhood and, while the first two shook the world to its core, it was the third that seemed to have the greatest effect on me. Christ, that makes me sound heartless, but don't underestimate just how significant this song is to me. Allow me to explain ...

The first time I heard the song 'Chains' by Tina (yes, I believe we are on a first-name basis, even though she has absolutely no idea who I am), the year was 1994 and I was eight. I was in a pivotal stage: I felt enamoured of the strong women in my life and confused as to why men seemed to be running the world. (That stage of my life continues.) I was sitting in the back of a brand-new Toyota sedan that someone had won in a raffle, and Jurek was helping out by driving it to the winner's house. I had never been in a brand-new car before, and it was roughly one million times better than Clare, our peach Tarago. My two brothers, my sister and I gushed over how smooth the seatbelts were and how weird the leather seats felt on the backs of our thighs. We all talked loudly over the top of each other and craned our necks at the traffic lights, hoping the other cars would see just how flash we looked. I felt like we were in a super-rare Lamborghini, but I know now we were in a white Toyota sedan, an unmarked taxi, if you will.

Amy was in the front seat, as she always was because she claimed to get car sick and was also a lying, opportunistic bully. Amy was fiddling with all the new-age buttons until she found where the radio was ... and there she was: Tina.

My skin tingled as the beats began and her honeyed voice poured over me. I wondered if the car's speakers were just so good that music felt more magical, but I knew deep down that no matter how good the speakers were, it didn't take away from the fact that the song itself was life-changing. Baby, baby, Tina was in chains and I was all for it.

I fell silent for the entire song and the noise of my siblings faded behind Tina's feminine power. I realised my reaction must be how my mum's lesbian friend Mandy felt when she played KD Lang (over and over and over). As soon as the song finished, I missed it. I never thought this could happen to me, I never thought this is where I would be.

'Chains' became a core memory. As the middle child of five kids, I had to share absolutely everything in my life. My mum, my nan, my bedroom, my bunkbed, my school holidays, my hairbrush and, most devastatingly, the contents of my diary. (Not forgotten OR forgiven, Amy!) 'Chains' became mine – a song only I truly understood, even though I didn't really understand at the time exactly what I was understanding. It made sense to me, and it wasn't until I became a mother that I knew what eight-year-old me had been grasping on to so tightly.

After twenty months of Olive, the most brutal baby I'd ever seen, let alone created, I gave birth to Edith. She was much, much easier, with a cheeky smile and delicious fat thighs. As adorable as she was, she was still a newborn, and newborns are my least favourite flavour of baby.

Amy can't relate to this. She loved the newborn stage – their helplessness, their smell, their inability to leave. Not me. I find newborns relentless, exhausting and unrewarding, which, again, makes me sound like a wicked witch, but this is my book so shove it up your jumper.

Throughout my entire pregnancy with Edie, I found myself terrified of having a newborn again. Olive was still a cranky little soul, but slightly (and I stress *slightly*) more reasonable in her second year of life. I was convinced I was going to have the exact replica of Olive, which filled me with fear and guilt that I felt any negative feelings at all about my firstborn. If I had a dollar for every time I've felt guilty since becoming a mother, I would give Gina Rinehart a run for her money. Oh my god, if I could monetise shame, I'd have ninety-nine problems, but paying the Telstra bill wouldn't be one of them.

The first couple of weeks of Edie's life were pretty smooth sailing because Lukasz was on paternity leave and he was in charge of keeping Olive alive while I was in charge of keeping Edie alive. It felt fair and doable, but those two weeks quickly vanished and he was back to work again, leaving me with a moody tyrant and a chubby potato. I was alone with two babies. Christ almighty.

Also, can we have a moment for how bloody mental it is to suggest that two weeks of the other parent helping is enough before they return to work full-time? Who came up with that timeframe? Because I would like to have a word with them. A mate of mine, who had kids well before me, had a dreadful time of it because her husband worked in hospitality and he had to put in a leave request form ahead of time. So he took a stab in the dark when the baby would be born and asked for two weeks off after that. In a cruel twist of fate, the baby was two weeks overdue, so he spent the last two weeks of his wife's pregnancy twiddling his thumbs while she farted around the house, and when their daughter was born, he had to return to work the next day. Bonkers. Revolting. No, thank you.

For most people, being in charge of a one-year-old and a newborn feels impossible to imagine because it's damn near impossible to do. I know most people think it's impossible on account of so many people telling me, 'I don't know how you do it! I'd die!' Well, forgive me for being dramatic, but I *was* dying. One-year-olds and newborns are two different species – they drink different types of milk, they wear different nappies (but don't worry, they both wear nappies that you have to change heaps of times throughout the day), they cry a lot but about different things, they have different sleep schedules and you have to keep them alive all of the time. Impossible? Maybe not. Relentless? Definitely.

Each morning I watched Lukasz leave the house, my shoulders slumping under the weight of a shitty night's sleep and immeasurable responsibility. Every day seemed to be completely different and totally unpredictable, apart from the fact it was always, always, always really, really, really hard. Some of you might have found this stage of parenthood a walk in the park, and so did I, but in the more literal sense because if I wasn't juggling them at home, I was at the bloody buggery park.

Fuck, I hate the park. All parks. If I never see a park again, I'd be stoked. In fact, as I write this I am sitting at an indoor play centre deep in the industrial part of Melbourne suburbia, where a kid won't stop crying because another kid has the tricycle she wants and her mum is staring at her phone, hoping no one works out the screamer belongs to her. No grown-up here is having a good time, so we're all banned from judging each other even though that's exactly what we're doing to deflect our own guilt that we aren't doing crafts with our kids or teaching them French. These play centres are always in massive tin warehouses, so they're scorching in summer, freezing in winter and have acoustics that allow you to hear a kid fart 20 metres away, but not the person sitting across the sticky table from you who's trying to talk. They sell hot chips cooked in dirty oil from 9am and the people who work here spend their time either doing nothing at all or cleaning human shit from the top of the slide. You think I'm exaggerating, but I once watched a poor bastard in a synthetic polo shirt climb to the top of the play equipment and pick up a steaming turd only to have a woman complain to him that the place should be cleaner. Um ... he didn't lay the turd, lady!

I come to the indoor parks when I need to get some work done, like when I have to write emails or chip away at the overdue book I am contractually obliged to write. Ahem. It's a special kind of unhygienic chaos here, but at least the doors close and there's enough padding to make you feel like it's safe. This isn't to say I hate them more or less than outdoor parks. No, no, no, in fact I hate them *equally*. They're both hell on earth for me, and I do not use that term lightly. I hate parks with the fire of a thousand suns because not only are they death traps for children, but you often find yourself having to talk to another parent and pretend to be interested in their snotty kid when all you want to do is sit alone in your car in the Woolworths car park eating a rotisserie chook with your bare hands. Is that SO MUCH TO ASK?!

Every outdoor park has a swing that the kids fight over, creating awkward friction between exhausted parents giving each other tight smiles and saying loudly to their kid, 'That's okay, I know it was your turn and he pushed in, but maybe you'll be next.' Hell. By the way, why do parks have swings? They're the only thing at the park where the kids do fuck-all but it puts your shoulder out and drains the last of your energy, even though the entire point of the park was to get rid of enough of the kids' energy that they have a nap long enough for you to watch an entire episode of *Real Housewives of Sydney*. I fucking hate parks.

I didn't *always* hate parks. This loathing was a gift from motherhood; I can't remember even seeing one before I had kids. Did they exist before I had a baby? I don't think they did. They were just pockets of blissful space in each suburb where people drank craft beer and listened to Bon Iver. I truly am so sorry my pesky womb ruined that for everyone.

The park down the road from our house at the time was called Warr Park and, honestly, it was so aptly named (Merri-Bek Council: no notes). I would go there every morning after feeding the two small dependents completely different breakfasts and changing different-sized nappies. I had to go to the park within a certain window so the newborn could have a sleep in the pram and the one-year-old could burn enough energy that she would sleep when we got home and the newborn was awake. So good and easy. In fact, for years my life was just managing their sleep schedules and never actually sleeping myself. Have kids, they say.

Every morning was the same. I would miss newborn Edie's sleep window ever so slightly, so she would tip into being overtired and the park visit would involve pushing a screaming newborn while the toddler yelled at me for not pushing her on the swing. I would yell over to the one-year-old tyrant, 'Just give me a minute, your sister is very upset,' knowing full well she didn't understand the concept of 'a minute' let alone her 'sister'. Olive would scream louder, as would Edie, and I would be pushed into a deafening corner where I was fighting for my sanity. Literally.

I started taking headphones with me to drown out the noise I dragged to the park every morning, because the crying was a given. A good mum wouldn't wear headphones, I thought, but I had reached the point of sleep deprivation where I wasn't afraid of people thinking I was a bad mum – or was it that I already thought I was one? Hard to say at that point: no thoughts about myself were ever gentle.

One spring morning, I got to Warr Park ready for battle, and quickly shoved my headphones in. I knew that getting Edie to sleep or watching Olive enjoy herself would be fruitless because Edie was overtired. Sigh ... Edie kicked off and I pushed the pram over the tanbark, hoping it would eventually have the same effect the cobblestones had on Olive. It feels wild that we rock babies to sleep like that; I couldn't imagine anything worse than being moved or whacked on the bum to sleep. Babies make absolutely no sense to me, but you've probably worked that out by now. Anyway, it wasn't working. Edie was screaming so much that her sweet little face was bright red and her tiny mouth was wide open, exposing her perfect pink gums. It's so strange that you can be transfixed by how flawless they are even when you're tipping over the edge to madness. Meanwhile, Olive was strapped into the swing, yelling at me to push her, so I would walk screaming Edie in circles, and give my furious little Olive an almighty push as I walked past.

It was all in vain. Neither daughter seemed to be calming down, and the gentle rage that simmered just below the surface started to bubble over. I wasn't angry at the girls – I knew, even in my exhaustion, that they didn't know how hard they were being. I was angry at the situation, at the insurmountable task ahead of me that had no end date. I felt livid at how helpless and alone I was because it made no sense – all I did was help them, and I was never ever actually alone. People walking past never offered a helping hand, not that I would accept it, but I was furious that this was all my job, all of the fucking time, and each day seemed excruciatingly long and only slightly shorter than the nights that went on forever and ever. I was drowning in not only the gigantic responsibilities that come with having two extremely dependent babies but also my overwhelming rage. There never seemed to be any reprieve, and I couldn't fathom a time in my life when it would be easier. Worse still, I couldn't comprehend a world in which I could survive this for much longer. Their cries increased in volume, so I turned my music up ... at the exact right time. Tina. Tina Bloody Arena entered the chat. Thank fucking fuck.

'Chains' is a song that starts softly, but promises to take the wind out of you at the chorus, and this is exactly what I needed. The babies cried louder, and I turned the music up as I pushed the pram and occasionally the swing as hard as my shoulder would allow. The babies cried even louder, the fury soared through my body, and when I realised I couldn't turn Tina up any more, I found myself singing. I was singing softly through gritted teeth at the start, but as the song built in intensity, so did my voice, and I realised that I wasn't just singing to block out the noise, I was singing because finally the song made complete sense to me!

I never thought this would happen to me! I never thought this is where I would be! Baby (#1), baby (#2), I'M – IN – CHAINS!

I was singing so loudly, and there were people walking past on their way to their shitty office jobs. I used to see those people and feel sorry for them, but since having two babies I looked at these people trotting along to their miserable jobs and thought, 'Can I come, too?' As soon as the song finished, I replayed it. I replayed the song four times and sang so loudly that I could taste blood. I felt alive. I felt validated. I felt utterly and completely mad.

And, in the hellscape that was the park, I officially was.

THE NOISE

Four am alarm. I needed to wake to an alarm instead of the baby crying so that I might feel like I was in control of one part of my life. The birds hadn't started singing yet and I tiptoed down the stairs, trying desperately not to wake the girls. I flicked the kettle on, cursing it for being so loud, and wished our townhouse was just that little bit bigger – big enough for me to swing a cat or to have an hour to breathe by myself.

We worked hard to get the townhouse – months and months of dealing with real estate agents and coming second at auction, until this one in Brunswick came on the market and we paid $30k more than the vendor asked. I absolutely despise real estate agents, but that is neither here nor there; I just need it documented somewhere before I die in case any of my kids or grandkids think it's a profession they might look into, and wonder if they would have my blessing. They would not.

Our townhouse had two storeys – downstairs was open-plan living with a small kitchen and lounge room that we divided with a 1 metre square dining table. Upstairs was a poky bathroom and two bedrooms – well, more like one and a half bedrooms. We'd moved there from the miniature one-bedroom apartment on Lygon Street, which we'd rented before having kids was even on the cards – somewhere we thought we would live like carefree young lovers, with access to bars and restaurants where we'd become regulars and get new inspiration for all our overseas adventures. Less than a year after signing the lease on that apartment, we brought Olive home to it. Huge LOL.

When we moved in to the townhouse, our first 'real home', we were so up ourselves. Olive was four months old and she now had her own room to store things she didn't have any desire to use, like reasoning and her cot. We quickly had the carpets replaced and renovated the kitchen and bathroom to feel like it truly was our place. Because we compared it to our one-bedroom apartment, this place felt huge! We had two floors, for god's sake: we were practically in a mansion!

I'd scoured vintage shops and the internet for furniture that suited both Lukasz and me. When I met him, Lukasz owned a black metal-framed bed and a framed poster of the 2009 UK Reading Music Festival, headlined by Arctic Monkeys and Kings of Leon. So, really, we went with my style by throwing out his rank bed and popping his framed poster on the wall behind the front door. The man is good at a lot of things, like Excel spreadsheets, being the life of the party and getting strangers to instantly like him, but he is *not* good at interior design (and, while I'm here, he's also not good at volume control – please stop yelling, I am standing right in front of you).

In such a small space, I'd decided on small bursts of colour to inject a bit of life into it. I wanted it simple yet cheerful, so I had white hexagon tiles in the kitchen with blonde wood cabinets and a big teal bowl of fruit. I had bright orange chairs around our small dining table and teal cushions on our brown couch (they were a pop of colour, but they were mostly used to disguise gross things the kids spilled on it). I bought prints with geometric shapes in oranges, pinks and blues, as well as a massive overexposed print of a bright blue lake from New Zealand or somewhere in Scandinavia. I never thought to ask the lady from the shop – I didn't care where it was from, I just knew I needed to look deep into it when I needed an escape, which was often. I loved how I decorated that little home. It made me feel proud and accomplished, until it didn't.

It was here, in this place I'd immediately loved and trusted with my entire family, the place I'd decorated lovingly within our modest budget, the place I called our home ... It was here that The Noise began.

It began slowly, almost like it wasn't in the same suburb as me. A high-pitched ringing I assumed was just roadworks or maybe a housewife screaming all day from her depths of despair – you know, harmless, normal stuff. It was faint enough to ignore for a long time and I thought it would just fade away once I'd had enough sleep.

When I was pregnant with Edie, my body expanded and took up more space in our tiny home. I felt enormous and dreaded the sound of a newborn baby. My ears were still ringing from the early days of Olive. Could The Noise just be the aftermath of that? Kind of like when you go to see a loud movie, and when it's over, your ears take time to adjust to the silence, or when you're freezing and you climb into a warm bath and it physically hurts? The Noise felt like a constant reminder of how hard it might become again, and I willed it to soften.

We had been in the house just over a year before Edie came along and our mansion with three guests in it became a shoebox with four giants. How could such a teeny-weeny baby make everything change shape?

Over time, as the weight of motherhood settled into my bones, making the days harder and the nights longer, The Noise slowly grew louder and louder, creeping closer. It moved down my street and up my driveway, sliding under my freshly painted maroon front door and bouncing off the walls where my treasured prints hung proudly and Lukasz's music festival poster hung secretly. The Noise brought with it a heavy rock that rested on my chest and became heavier and heavier as the day went on. By night-time, the rock would be so heavy that my breathing became short and fast and I would be out of breath making dinner.

Over the months, any space I thought we'd had started to shrink and our things became cumbersome. The pram we had by the door began to feel like a horse and carriage that I needed to straddle to get into the kitchen, and the dining table felt like it was there solely for me to stub my toes on.

With Lukasz working and me trying to survive a toddler and a newborn, this beautiful little home morphed into another beast to fight. It didn't help that we had a psychotic neighbour named Bree who, when one of the girls cried, would smash her fists on the shared walls and scream, 'Shut the fuck up!' One time she demanded I move my laundry basket from the shelf in my courtyard because she could *see it* from her courtyard. I was so fed up with her bullying that I said no, so she ran upstairs, put her speakers next to my daughters' bedroom, where they were asleep, and blasted Evanescence so loudly that the walls shook. The only thing louder than the 'Bring Me To Life' chorus was The Noise. Bree's god-awful energy, lack of empathy and downright arseholery only amplified The Noise I was trying to keep at bay. Thanks to Bree, I had yet another reason to try to keep my kids from crying – a fully grown woman who hated the sound of children yet willingly chose to live in a densely populated suburb popular with families. If I ever see that woman again, I will tell her to go fuck herself. There aren't many people in this world I loathe, but that piece of shit is one of them. Bree, if you're reading this: fuck you.

At 4.15am, I sat at my dining table and pulled out the gigantic stack of essays on *The Crucible* that my Year 12 English students wrote. I sipped my coffee and tried to ignore the gentle early signs of The Noise, and the rock that sat softly on my chest. The Noise sounded like a combination of a boiling kettle, slamming cupboards, a buzzing phone and a crying baby. By this stage, I had been living with it for months, but I knew it was soft enough in the mornings for me to mark essays swiftly. As the hours piled up, The Noise would ramp up and I found the only way I could soften it was if I was louder than it.

I became a caricature of myself, speaking loudly in streams of consciousness to anyone who would listen. Hell, I think I spoke to a lot of people who didn't listen, but I don't blame them. My cheeks flush with humiliation as I think of those days of filling space with my booming voice in the hope The Noise wouldn't follow me. I feel sorry for the teachers who shared an office with me; they were accosted every time I was there. I was on such a tangent one day that one teacher looked up at me and said, 'I watched a movie on the weekend about war. Bron, your voice reminds me of a machine gun.' The other teachers burst out laughing as if someone had addressed something they were too polite to acknowledge themselves, like an eye-watering fart in an Uber.

It didn't slow me down, though. I charged around the school, from class to class and then back to my office, where my colleagues/victims sat nervously awaiting my return. Even after that machine-gun comment,

I had absolutely no idea how insufferable I was or how insanely I was presenting until one of the teachers, the senior psychology teacher, asked if I was up for a psych assessment. I figured he was asking everyone, so I agreed and followed him outside to a table near the canteen, chatting his ear off the whole way.

The questions started, and I soon realised what was happening. This wasn't a random test, this was him trying to show me, in the kindest way possible, that he didn't think I was mentally okay. My skin stung with embarrassment. How long had he thought this? Did everyone think this? I fudged my way through most of the questions, downplaying how dramatically overwhelmed I felt 100 per cent of the time, and he ticked the boxes without making any eye contact. I felt stitched up, especially when he read the question 'Do you think you could be a successfu stand-up comedian?' I'd just started doing open-mic nights at comedy gigs, so the answer was 'Yes, more than likely', but I felt sheepish saying that. I realised that he thought I was so manic that I imagined myself brilliant enough to do stand-up, which was utterly humiliating. I was like that demented old lady from mum's work at the nursing home who thought she was the Queen of England. It dawned on me, at that table outside the canteen, that I was a walking joke at my work, and I wanted to crawl into a hole and never come out. The Noise got louder, and I desperately tried to accept it, but it felt like ants crawling on my skin.

As ashamed as I was, I weighed up my options: stay loud, big and insufferable, or let The Noise swallow me whole. If I didn't have two small kids at home, I probably would have chosen the latter, but I didn't have that luxury, so the self-inflicted humiliation continued. I walked back to the office, biting my tongue, holding in the outbursts I had become so accustomed to delivering. The self-restraint didn't last long, and I continued to torment that office until the madness subsided, and I can't even remember when or if that happened while I was working there. I don't think it did. I do remember hoping that was the last of the psych tests a colleague would put me through. To this day I don't know the results of that test – I imagine they weren't in my favour and he kept them to himself as a professional courtesy. Maybe, just maybe, I nailed it and I was more sane then than I've ever been, but the chances of that are about as slim as my seventy-two-year-old mum having another baby.

And thus, I continued to create a life that was louder than any kettle, cupboard door, phone or baby's cry. I created a life that was fast and uncomfortable and exhausting because the only thing worse than sprinting and yelling was sitting still and letting The Noise swallow me whole.

At 5.30 am I put my essays away and, instead of creeping back into bed, where I could wait for my girls to wake for the day, I walked out the door to fight The Noise head-on with the thing that almost blew my family to bits: fucking CrossFit.

SHRINK, GIRL! SHRINK!

At 5.30 am most mums with tiny babies are scrambling around the house heating up milk or cuddling a sleep-drenched toddler, but not me. I was storming towards my car in the freezing Melbourne winter with a determination I had never experienced. It didn't even compare to when I was nineteen and got green contact lenses and tried doggedly to convince friends they mustn't have noticed how green my eyes were before.

When Olive was one and Edie was two months old, I needed an outlet. As cute as these two babies were, it was confronting to realise that for the next seven months of maternity leave, at all times, I would be holding at least one of them. The Noise was seeping into more hours of my day and I put it down to exhaustion. Surely every tired parent can hear it, I thought. I hoped my awful neighbour Bree could hear it, but she seemed to only ever hear my kids being kids, which was apparently hell on earth for her.

I hadn't brought up The Noise with Lukasz because it wasn't loud enough to feel real yet, plus it was still so early in our relationship that I wanted him to think I was everything he wanted in a partner. You remember the early stages, when you don't fart in front of each other or you pretend you know who George Washington is? Or you say you have never wet the bed as an adult, only once in Sri Lanka but that wasn't your fault? You can relate, I'm sure. Well, Lukasz and I had a baby and another baby so fast that we were still learning about each other and I wanted him to think I was perfect for just a little bit longer. So The Noise remained my problem.

Lukasz worked full-time in an office (remember when people did that?) and his hours were long. I would send him videos all day of the girls at the park, or at the library, or just eating a delicious lunch. I thought I was doing it to make him feel included, but if I'm honest I think it was probably to prove how much I was doing. I will never come to terms with how much work has to be done to keep a human baby alive and safe, so those videos acted as evidence that I, like most mothers of tiny children, was doing just that, on my own, for most of the day. Resentment can curdle even the sweetest of moments.

I still had whiplash from Olive's first year of life, so staring down the barrel of another first year of life, as well as learning how to deal with a toddler, was sobering. When Lukasz's paternity leave dried up, I felt trapped. I needed to concoct a plan to get myself out of the house on my own every so often. Unfortunately, the only acceptable thing for a mother of small babies to do alone was to get back in shape. What? You don't believe me? Have a little think back to when you were growing up. Did your mother have hobbies she left the house for that didn't look like exercise? As if. And if she did, I bet your mum is an absolute baller. My mum didn't go anywhere except work, which is why we grew up so filthy rich (*cough cough*). The only reason exercise is an exception to this rule is that at least the woman is acknowledging her responsibility to satisfy the male gaze and trim right back to the smallest physical version of herself. If she does that, we can dress it up as 'self-care' and 'female empowerment'. Everyone wins! (Except most women, who would much prefer to go to the movies alone and eat a boysenberry choc-top instead of boot camp but, honestly, who's asking them?)

I nervously attended a trial CrossFit class with Claire, whose baby girl, Stevie, was the same age as Olive. For all the normal people out there, CrossFit is a cult-like fitness regimen that focuses on weightlifting and excruciating workouts. The first half of the class is usually lifting enormous weights as if it's a normal thing to do, and the second half is a WOD (Workout of the Day) that involves gymnastics and extreme cardio that gives you flashbacks to your high school cross country, even though you'd forged your stepdad's signature on a note about why you needed to sit it out. The classes were an hour of physical endurance that teetered on torture, but they were an entire hour away from my life as I knew it, so I absolutely loved it.

Claire had read about it somewhere and was certain it was the answer to all our problems/body dysmorphia. On the way to the class we pumped each other up, joking about how strong we were going to be, but knowing each other well enough to understand that all we really wanted was to be hot. The trial class wasn't as hard as we thought it was going to be so, high on endorphins, we both signed up to attend three classes a week. We were invigorated by reclaiming our bodies, but even more so by the prospect of three whole hours outside of our house sans kids. I mean, not actually alone – technically we would be in a room with twenty people we had nothing in common with, physically walloping ourselves, often to the point of injury, but we wouldn't be anyone's mother in that time. For three separate sixty-minute windows, no one would ask us to pick them up, to change a nappy or to clean food or vomit off the floor and, most importantly, we wouldn't feel entrenched in the monotonous boredom that comes with motherhood. It's a boredom no one warns you about, a boredom you feel guilty about feeling, and a boredom that makes you question every life decision you've ever made.

At the beginning of our CrossFit initiation, Claire and I would huddle next to each other and scoff at all the middle-aged people rolling around on the floor stretching before class. These people were unencumbered by shame, and it stunned us. Surely they weren't taking this *that* seriously? It was just a dumb fitness class, it wasn't the bloody Olympics! We would call each other on our drive home and laugh loudly about how stupid some of the exercises were and how embarrassing it was when people applauded others when they completed a workout or lifted something heavy. The whole thing seemed so patronising and humiliating, and yet we kept going.

For a few months, Claire and I attended religiously, until she grew bored of it and quit. Claire does that. She is the queen of fads: F45, barre, pottery, meditation, painting – each and every one of them is 'life-changing' for her until it isn't, and I love that about her. CrossFit was a notch on her belt of failed fads, but for me it was different. I had taken to it like a duck to water, a moth to a flame, a mother to a boysenberry choc-top. It was a place where The Noise quietened, which meant it became my place of solitude. I splurged on bright new exercise gear and found myself looking forward to the classes like they were Christmas. Soon, three classes a week wasn't enough, so I bumped up my membership to 'unlimited classes' and went every single morning, and sometimes secretly again in the afternoon.

The owner of the CrossFit 'box' (they're not gyms, okay, they're boxes: never ever make that mistake with a CrossFitter; they'll relish correcting you and you will roll your eyes so hard that they will fall out of your skull, trust me) approached me one morning and suggested I take the next morning off to give my body a rest. At the time, I took it personally. I assumed she thought I was getting too much bang for my buck, but in hindsight she was totally right. It wasn't yet clear to me that I had developed an addiction to lifting weights and thrashing my body until I could taste blood; that realisation came years later. Twice I hurt my back so badly that I couldn't walk without wincing, and turning in bed made my eyes water, but I still showed up to that 6am class. Every. Single. Day.

There were a number of reasons why I loved it. Let's address the vain element first – I looked incredible. I was lean and muscular with arms that didn't wobble and a firm, perky bum. For the first time in my life, I looked at my body in the mirror and loved it entirely. I know that sounds like I was totally up myself, but it was wild to spend my whole life envious of people who loved their bodies and then finally achieve it. I acted shy when people at the box said, 'I can't believe you have two kids and look like that!' I'd say, 'What? Don't be silly!' while thinking, 'Me fucking either. I had no idea my body was even capable of looking like this! Let's all take a moment to appreciate it.'

My activewear collection grew and I became fixated on my body. I knew I looked amazing, but it was hard to ignore the possibility of reaching perfection. There is something intoxicating about successfully getting smaller when you've spent your life failing to do so. Thanks to growing up as a human female in western culture, I'd been bombarded with ideas of what the perfect woman looked like. Mum's collection of

Woman's Day magazines meant there was always a selection of shamed women with cellulite to tut-tut over and svelte women who had lost weight to celebrate. The smaller women were always interviewed and all of the questions focused on their weight-loss secrets, which meant that only women who had shrunk got a voice.

As I grew from child to teenager to adult, I played the socially acceptable role of pretending to embrace my body and shun the public demands on women to shrink; but I am a product of my time. I wanted to be thin, and I made countless empty promises to myself to deprive myself of food and to exercise more. I feel dejected as I reflect on all the years I have wasted hating my body and, trust me, there are days when I pinch my stomach fat and mentally list all the 'bad choices' I've made and what I have 'let myself' eat, so really I'm not sure if I've learnt a fucking thing, but I hope I have. I don't know if we were getting anywhere with the body positivity movement, but considering how popular Ozempic has been with people who don't medically need it, it seems to me like we have obliterated any progress that movement made. As much as I tell my daughters to love their bodies (and yes, eventually my son) exactly the way they are, if a repulsive gremlin crawled out of a drain covered in human shit with a lifetime supply of Ozempic, I would grab it with both hands and chalk myself up as the luckiest woman alive. The allure of being small seems unrelenting, and the older I get, the more I doubt it will ever stop.

I grew up with the undeniable message that small was good. With all the physical training, it was easy for me to deprive myself of 'bad' foods. I became so addicted to people complimenting my body that I found myself completely cutting out carbs and sugar to shrink even more and collect compliments as if they were currency. Once I was thin, I felt like

I had solved a riddle – I had bloody done it! I had found the 'cure' to my 'battle with the bulge', and I sank my teeth into it with the promise that I would never go back to how I looked before CrossFit (which was just a 'regular'-looking woman, by the way. How awful *eye roll*).

A severe back injury finally put a stop to my CrossFit days, and it was a blessing in disguise. While I am glad I got to see what living in a body like that felt like, I don't miss that chapter of my life for a second. The price I paid to achieve that snatched little bod was far, far too high and, if I could, I'd go back in time and never ever go to that first CrossFit class. I would drive Claire to the movies, buy us both boysenberry choc-tops and tell our families we went to Pilates.

But I don't have the luxury of changing my past; I can only write a book about how much shame I feel about that time and hope it graces me with a semblance of self-forgiveness. I'm not hopeful.

And yet, I push on.

EXERCISING MY WAY TO OBLIVION

Being thin wasn't the only reason I went to CrossFit. I loved it because there was a start and an end to the class, unlike every other part of my life. Having a newborn and a toddler at the same time felt like I was juggling sacred vases while a Jack Russell nipped at my ankles. Don't get me wrong, I have always loved those baby girls more than anything in the whole world, but you can love your babies without loving all of the hours you need to spend with them. It was so unbelievably hard, and there was always, always, always something to cook, something to clean, somewhere to go and a foul smell I couldn't find. I now know it was Lukasz's breath all along. BOOM! (Just kidding, Lukasz – I'm just making sure you read this book.)

Recently I did a gig with a Sydney comedian who had a new baby. He looked like he had been hit by a car, and he said, 'I don't know how you've had three. Just one baby is killing me.' I smiled and thought, 'Just one almost killed me too. I think I've almost died a million times since becoming a mother.'

CrossFit gave me achievable goals, whereas motherhood didn't. I could see a weight I wanted to lift and, with enough practice, I'd lift it, and not only lift it but receive applause for doing so. There is a real cult vibe to CrossFit, and I lived and breathed it like a woman with a bandana and incredible fertility. When someone got their first pull-up it was as exciting as when I got my first pull-up. The box would erupt with glee because Paul ran the block without stopping, or Jan got her first toes-to-bar or Donna lifted her first 100-kilogram deadlift. Everyone's ability was different, from chubby sixty-five-year-old women who lifted pretend weights to machines, freaks of nature, who could lift double their weight and throw their muscular bodies above a pull-up bar as if they were made of elastic. Everyone's wins felt both life-changing and deeply personal and we celebrated them as if they were the only things that mattered.

One box I went to had a big cow bell on the wall, and when someone got a new PB (personal best, omg, please keep up, non-CrossFitters), they would be encouraged to ring it. I remember watching a man throw a barbell above his bright red head as his sweaty body shook violently under the weight of it. His elbows looked like they were going to snap and his eyes bulged out of his face like a cartoon character seeing a sexy lady. He couldn't have looked more frightened if he tried, and as he threw the heavy bar down, slamming the weights into the padded floor, the gym erupted and a beaming trainer with a tidy haircut pushed him towards the cow bell. He sheepishly rang it and people cheered louder and, even though I had officially drunk the Kool-Aid by then, this act made me go bright red. The last time I'd felt so embarrassed was when I was heavily pregnant with Olive and the lady at Bakers Delight in Barkly Square asked me in front of a bunch of people if I was ever going to buy something or was I just going to eat the free samples every day? Silly bitch, as if I'm ever going to buy something when you're literally giving it away for free.

When the classes were over, I would go home, high on endorphins, the sound of applause still fresh in my mind. I would walk in the door and Lukasz would be feeding our tiny girls breakfast at the tiny dining table. Their little faces would light up when they saw me, a vision I will never tire of. A wave of remourse for not being there when they woke up would wash over me, and I would shake that off by rushing to take over the domestic tasks. I kept telling myself that I deserved an hour for myself, even if I didn't really believe it.

For four long years I gave my mornings to CrossFit. My girls grew bigger and they didn't remember the mother I was before it. In fact, I couldn't remember her either. I grew physically stronger and my relationship with Lukasz became strained. He had no interest in fitness, which was actually a relief. I wanted this all to myself – I just needed one thing, and CrossFit felt sacred. People there knew me as an impressive athlete, not as a mum or a teacher or the lady who made sure there was food in the fridge. It felt like a place where I could focus on me and be celebrated for that, whereas in every other part of my life I took a back seat, just a woman and The Noise. Being a mother is relentless, and being a teacher is the same. At home I felt like I could never get on top of the cleaning, and at work I felt like I could never get on top of all the god-awful essay marking. Re. Lent. Less.

As hard as the workouts were, life outside of the box was more gruelling. As soon as I left the box, I would sprint from responsibility to responsibility, letting everyone down in varying degrees. I couldn't seem to move fast enough to feel like I was making a dent in all of the things people expected of me, whereas at CrossFit, I was soaring! I was greeted with smiles from the other CrossFitters who quickly became my closest friends, despite knowing hardly anything about me, and vice versa. I liked that they knew almost nothing about me. They didn't know how many brothers and sisters I had, where I was born, that my ripped body was just as new to me as it was to them or that I was struggling to keep my head above water all day, every bloody day.

I threw myself into those new friendships to the point of embarrassment, and it was easy to do. Thanks to the endorphins, the fact that no one outside of the box could possibly understand how important CrossFit was to me, and that I had no time to see most of my actual friends, the relationships with some of the CrossFitters were formed on steroids. (Well, not steroids, CrossFitters don't do that, just low GI protein bars). If I went to a social event, it would be with them, and we kept finding new ways to hang out. I'm sure those relationships were normal for everyone else there, innocent and peripheral friendships that they could add to their real ones, but I went all-in, hungrily, as if desperately building a new life outside the exhausting one I already had. (Again, it shames me to even think about this, let alone put it on paper, but I promised myself I would be honest in this book otherwise what's the point of writing it?) I loved CrossFit because I felt admired there. I felt successful, strong, brilliant and sexy compared to my real life, where I felt tired, useless, unimpressive and invisible.

And so I went. A lot. Rain, hail, shine, sleep, no sleep, injury, no injury, I went. I would get up at 4am to mark essays, and zip out the door at 5.30 to see all my new friends, who had become my ticket to feeling more than just a mum and a teacher. I know now that I was grasping at straws for a win, any win, but at the time CrossFit felt so important that, without it, I would have crumbled under the weight of the life I'd worked so hard to build.

I had no idea until ages after I finished CrossFit that I wasn't there to better myself. It took me years to put the pieces together. My undiagnosed postnatal anxiety had created a hurricane of chaos. I would thrash myself, trying to exert any energy I had left so I might have a fighting chance of getting to sleep at night and bypassing the negative self-talk. I couldn't hear The Noise when I was working out, which was another drawcard. The Noise grew louder and louder as the day went on and would override everything if I slowed down for even a minute. So I didn't slow down.

There were a bunch of reasons I went to CrossFit, but I think I know the underlying one. I've had enough time away from it to truly understand why I would go every single day, sometimes twice. It wasn't only for the new friendships, in which I could pretend I was someone completely different, or to escape my life or The Noise or to battle the voice that told me I was a complete fuck-up. It wasn't only to achieve the body I always thought I wanted or for people to praise me for achieving it. It was because it hurt. It physically hurt, and I believed at that point in my life that this was exactly what I deserved.

I got the lean and muscular body I thought I'd always wanted within a couple of months of starting because I went at it like my life depended on it, and it truly felt like it did. Every workout I would push my body to the brink, straining every muscle, threatening the very structure of my spine and splitting the skin on the palms of my hands. I hated myself so intensely during that time of my life that I would punish myself and mask it as 'self-care'. The self-hatred was offset by the admiration I felt from my new 'friends', and my anxious brain would tell me that the only place I felt good was where I was smashing my body into oblivion.

I dread to think about what I looked like from the perspective of my real friends and family. It was such an aggressive shift from how I'd lived my life, so it must have been as confusing as when Celine Dion wore a suit backwards. Apart from Lukasz, I can't remember any of them ever saying anything negative about it. Nothing to really challenge me on it anyway. They must have thought that because I wasn't crying into a pillow or drinking gin at breakfast, surely I was okay. In fact, some of them would have thought I was more than okay – at times I was ecstatic. I spoke too loudly and too much and I wore clothes that showed off my new body. I was nailing life, right? But I was not okay. I was burning my life down from the inside because my brain told me I didn't deserve it.

It took a severe back injury to stop me going to CrossFit and, while I thought I was disappointed, deep down I was relieved it was finally over. Four years of pushing myself physically and begging the universe to hurt me. Four years of missing my girls waking up in the morning. Four years of giving my relationship with poor Lukasz next to nothing. I risked absolutely everything during that stage of my life and, while Lukasz and I can kind of laugh about it now, it still feels tender. I don't think I've ever had a truly honest conversation with him about it, because in the process of hurting myself, I hurt him immeasurably.

I'll never forgive myself for that.

AVOIDING THE DREADED DOCTOR

I haven't really had a great run with GPs. No one ever visits them when things are going well and, in my case, most of the times I saw one it was for a prescription that pharmacists should really be able to give out, such as antibiotics, anti-nausea wafers and a judgemental tone. What makes visiting GPs even worse is that in the history of the world there has never ever been a nice medical receptionist. This means you turn up feeling awful only to be chastised by some lady with huge acrylic nails and a general disdain for people who don't remember their doctor's name because they see a different one every damn time.

One hundred per cent of my GP visits start like this:

'Uh, hi, I have an appointm—'

A finger with a large acrylic nail shoots up to silence me, followed by some click-clacking on the keyboard as the receptionist squints at the screen, offering no indication of when she will speak to me. Should I sit down? Should I leave? Should I apologise for existing?

'Right,' she sighs, making sure not to look up at me. 'Name?' I hesitate because she could be speaking to anyone. Is she speaking to someone on the phone through her Madonna headset? 'Name?!' She asks impatiently.

'Oh, sorry, Bronwyn Lewis,' I mumble, trying hard not to show that her rudeness is getting the better of me.

'And?'

'And I have an appointment.' My skin prickles. I speak quietly because the waiting room is always eerily quiet, filled with sick people and people desperate to hear someone confess to the receptionist the embarrassing reason they are there.

'Good for you,' she says sarcastically. 'Who with?' She finally looks up at me over her thick red-framed glasses. She looks as if I've just come in to tell her I've given her a parking ticket, which in turn makes my whole body stiffen.

'Sorry,' I say, 'I don't know their name. I just booked in with whoever had space.' I can feel myself stumbling through my words like I've been busted wagging. I regret coming. Maybe I can ride this out at home?

She looks back down at her screen and the acrylic nails click-clack away furiously. 'Right, let me check, then. Let's see, let's see ... Briony, was it?'

'No, Bronwyn. Bronwyn Lewis.'

'Oh, you remember your name, don't you.' Her nails are still frantically tapping away. She thinks her passive aggression can be taken as humour, but I'm in no mood, and even if I was, she's not funny. *clack clack clack* What the fuck could she possibly be writing? My patience runs out. I want to leave before I tell her she's a rude bitch, but I need to see this doctor for a prescription a pharmacist should be able to give me. I can feel all the other people in the waiting room watching me, which only makes me more annoyed.

'Sorry, why are you be—'

'Doctor Turner.' She cuts me off. 'Take a seat.'

Every. Damn. Time. I bloody hate medical receptionists. I think they do a short course in How to Simultaneously Master Both Disdain and Apathy. No other profession can manage it, except maybe the car registry office. I wonder if they have joint Christmas parties?

I grew up with a mum as a nurse (I think Hels prefers 'nurse as a mum') and anyone who grew up with a mum/nurse knows that none of their sicknesses or injuries were ever real. I once broke my wrist and it took a whole week of wailing in the bottom of my bunk bed for her to take me to get an X-ray. Mum's approach to our sicknesses created five people who hate going to the doctor. One of my brothers became a doctor himself, which I imagine feels like he's playing dress-ups in some weird pantomime every day. How embarrassing for him. I wonder if he'll ever get a real job?

Like all nurse/mums, our mum fobbed off a lot of our injuries or illnesses, which gave me and my siblings the clear message that our bodies and minds were fine if we just ignored them enough. Unfortunately, nurse/mums also ignore their own illnesses, which meant we grew up with a mum who, for days, ignored her broken thumb after doing the worm at my little brother's twenty-first and, worse still, her crumbling mental health. Having a nurse/mum was also one of the greatest gifts I've been given – I am far more resilient because of her – but I would be remiss if I didn't wonder whether her steely 'she'll be right' approach shot us all – including herself – in the foot (an injury she would have rinsed under the tap and slapped a bandaid on). I wonder if she wonders the same thing.

I thought my teenage years of helplessly watching my mum spiral and disregard her need for medical intervention were the worst it could get for me, but they weren't. The price I paid for Mum's approach to her mental health came many years later, when I became a mother myself. It turned me from a minor character in someone else's narrative of mental shortcomings to the main character in my own shitty story, whose audience was no longer me and my siblings but my own children. Zero stars, I do not recommend that play.

My distrust of GPs isn't only because Mum seldom took us; it's because they always make me feel like whatever is wrong with me is my fault (and sometimes it is, but save the lecture, sweetheart). That OR they're weirdos. When I was twenty I went to the strangest GP for the first (and last) time. I was there to get a prescription a pharmacist should have been able to give me, so I was anticipating being in her sterile, joyless examination room for two minutes max. Dr Creep scribbled my request onto the prescription pad, but threw a spanner in the works by asking when I had my last pap smear. I had never had a pap smear, which blew Dr Creep's tiny mind. She huffed and she puffed and she blew her disappointment all over me while I sat in my chair like a naughty little girl who had just been caught drawing on the walls with her own shit. Without giving me an option, she told me to remove my pants so she could smear me quick smart. Awful.

I cannot stress enough how much I didn't want to do it. Not only had I heard nightmare reviews of the blasted things, but I was so unprepared for this surprise invasion that it was a million times worse. I felt tricked. I wanted to stand up and walk straight out of Dr Creep's office but, as mentioned, I was twenty years old, which is basically fourteen years old, so I smiled and agreed as if an impromptu poke around in my cervix was exactly what I wanted. Let's fucking go, Dr Creep!

I went behind the curtain and took off my jeans and undies and sat on the bed dressed like Winnie the Pooh. I was shivering from both the cold and the shock at having to do something so invasive without warning. I wanted to run out of there and google what to expect when getting a pap smear, but I was stuck between a curtain and my new level of feminine shame. Dr Creep aggressively drew back the curtain and said, 'I can't believe you've been so complacent with your pap smears. I bet you've never had a breast exam either, have you?' I gulped. I had not. Fuck. She rolled her eyes and said, 'Okay, off with your shirt and bra.'

I should have grabbed my pants and run out of there, but I was so stunned and so half naked that I just told myself that the sooner I did what she asked, the sooner it would be over and done with. So I took my top off, and unclasped my bra and stood there, freezing cold, in a room I'd never been in, with a stranger I had only just met, COMPLETELY NUDE. Yep, within ten minutes of being in the room, I found myself on a bed with a complete stranger, BUCK NAKED, while she shoved things in me and grabbed my tits for way longer than a normal tit exam goes for. It was like the end of a bad date and I had a million alarm bells going off, which I had to ignore because I was the patient, she was the doctor and this discomfort and lack of autonomy was the cost of being a woman.

I vividly remember the feeling of Dr Creep's hands on my boobs, and her equipment up my fudga, as I desperately tried to disassociate. I clenched my eyes shut and tried to breathe my way through it. I kept reminding myself, 'She is a doctor, this is not a weird thing that's happening. She's a woman, women don't do weird things. Breathe, Bron,' but I knew this wasn't normal. I doubt she was getting a sexual kick out of it – in fact, there was nothing sexy about it – but it still felt predatory. I was unbelievably vulnerable, and quite obviously terrified, but she just kept demanding more access to my body and I kept silently allowing it.

Not once did she ask me if this was something I was okay with, nor did she check to see if I was okay or if I wanted a sheet to cover my naked body.

I hate that I didn't challenge her on any of this, but I know why I didn't. For those wondering if I overreacted or misread a perfectly normal interaction with a trained medical professional, please know that it has almost been twenty years since this appointment and I still tense up at the thought of it. I can remember the smell of her perfume, the touch of her cold hands and the feeling of dread she filled me with. I've since had a number of breast exams and pap smears (brag), and never ever have the doctors made me feel as trapped or as tricked as this one did. Both breast exam and pap smear were never done at the same time and they were always suggested delicately for a future date rather than demanded of me immediately.

I was a twenty-year-old woman, which some might assume is old enough to speak up if things feel a bit off, but I'd lived twenty years as a female, which means I'd lived two decades with an abundantly clear message that my body didn't actually belong to me. Twenty years of consuming telly shows that objectified and dismissed women, twenty years of bearing witness to heinous news reports of women being brutally murdered, and twenty years of feeling like whatever happened to my body was my fault for simply being a woman.

When Dr Creep finally told me I could put my clothes back on, I felt dirty and ashamed, and that feeling lingered for fucking ages. I walked into the waiting room and felt convinced that everyone in there was embarrassed for me. As I paid the moll medical receptionist, she asked if I wanted to make any follow-up appointments, and I blurted out, 'No way!'

She looked up at me, perhaps the only time she made eye contact with anyone for the day, and said, 'Okay, well, you don't have to be so rude about it.'

I should have told her to get fucked, but I was twenty, again, basically fourteen, so I quickly apologised. I hate that I apologised.

I don't have many memories of seeing the GP growing up, and I saw them even less after my visit to Dr Creep. My mum/nurse knew how to look after her kids perfectly well until her brain betrayed her, and her reluctance to take GPs seriously planted in my brain a seed of distrust towards the medical world. Dr Creep helped that seed flourish into a gigantic oak tree that stood firmly in front of logic. This combination was so damaging as my life progressed, because as I started to lose my mind (honestly, who saw that coming?), I avoided GPs as best I could. That was until I met a GP who tricked me in a way that saved my life.

DO YOU THINK YOU'RE A GOOD MOTHER?

I was hanging out the washing one day as the girls played in the backyard. They were two and three years old by this stage and my CrossFit addiction was in full swing. The sun was shining and I added 'Go to the park' to my gigantic mental list of things to do that day. Clamping a peg on the exercise leggings I had worn only hours earlier, I thought, with a flash of pride, 'Wow, I've already washed this morning's dirty laundry. I'm absolutely nailing this!'

This sense of accomplishment was interrupted by email notifications on my phone. I had roughly one million essay drafts in my inbox, each from a student who was demanding feedback faster than a spill in the Liberal Party. The endorphins from my morning workout were wearing off and The Noise was starting to ramp up, like violent diarrhoea in Bali: unwelcome but expected. I searched my brain for a solution to both marking essays and looking after the girls that day. Between the essays and keeping the girls alive, I was always rushing. There were never enough hours in the day and the girls weren't yet old enough to understand that I needed an hour of quiet time to work. So I marked whenever there was a silent moment: at 4–5.30 am and 8–10.30 pm. The night-time marking was like pushing shit uphill because I was exhausted from the day and I'd almost certainly had a couple of gin and tonics while cooking dinner to dull The Noise.

As I played mental Tetris with my tasks for the day, I noticed I had run out of pegs. I looked around and saw two-year-old Edie throwing them over the fence. Immediately frustrated, I said, 'Edie!' Which frightened her so much that she started crying. Awash with guilt as I tried to comfort her, I heard Olive start to cry – not because I had frightened her, but because she had climbed into a bucket of rainwater and her favourite skirt was now saturated. I had both girls climbing all over me, half a basket of damp clothes and an inbox full of unmarked essays. The Noise ramped up. My throat tightened. My phone pinged. I glanced down and it was a text from a friend.

How's your day going? she asked.

You know, I typed. *Same old, same old.*

You're lucky you have so much going on!

Fuck off.

Lucky? I wrote. *I hate my life.*

When she didn't reply straight away, The Noise grew even louder. *I mean, who doesn't hate their life? Ha ha! It's normal!* I was attempting to lighten the mood.

Heaps of people, Bron. I think it's normal to like your life.

I slammed my phone down. There it was. Yet another indicator I was getting it wrong. I had misread the situation and, instead of a mutual rant about how relentless life was, I was punched in the face with judgement. Well, that's how I saw it. How dare this woman tell me how to feel when all I ever did was make sure everyone else felt okay?

When did *my* feelings suddenly become important?

I furiously charged on with the day, handwashing Olive's skirt, making lunches, marking half an essay, doing the grocery shopping, vacuuming, marking half an essay, folding the washing, cooking dinner, giving the girls a bath, and the whole time that sentence thrashed around my brain: 'It's normal to like your life.'

The next morning, I worked out harder than ever, trying to shake the feeling that sentence gave me, but it hung around like pungent onion breath on a date. Why did I hate my life so much when from the outside it looked pretty great?

'Mate, I think you need to see a doctor,' Claire said to me.

'No, thanks!' I said, pouring her another wine.

'I knew you would say that, but I reckon if you tell a GP how you're feeling, they might be able to help you.'

The very idea annoyed me. What was the GP going to do? Mark the essays? Clean my bathroom? Ridiculous.

'Aren't you curious to see if they can help you feel less ... angry?' This made me even more furious than before. It dawned on me that I was almost always angry. If I wasn't riding a high from CrossFit, I was livid about something, ranging from a fourteen-year-old turd calling me 'a fucking ugly cunt' at school to finding a speck of pasta sauce still on a dish after washing it with the expensive dishwashing tablets. Everything felt like a personal attack, and when you're a high school teacher, a lot of your days consist of them. I felt like molten lava was coursing through my veins and lived in fear of exploding in the face of someone who didn't expect it. I guess anyone would become cranky if they had The Noise in their head most of the time. All I wanted was some fucking silence and extra hours in the day. Was that so much to ask?!

After over a decade of friendship, Claire could read me better than my mum could read an article about Bec Hewitt in *Woman's Day*, so after a few days of fighting it, I booked an appointment at the local GP. I had very little hope she would be able to help me, but when you're on a sinking ship in the middle of the Atlantic, you still yell 'HELP!' I wonder what the billionaires in the submarine yelled before they imploded. Whatever it was, I'm sure for a split second they experienced what postnatal anxiety feels like. Despite never having been a billionaire or in a submarine, I reckon their situation is the closest comparison I can muster. Respectfully.

The GP was a woman in her forties with a blazer and a blonde bob. I wondered why she was dressed for court, but I was in exercise gear, so she was probably wondering why I was dressed for a Jane Fonda costume party. She got straight to the point, which I appreciated.

'Good to meet you, Bronwyn. What brings you in today?' She kept her eyes on her computer screen and I hoped with all my raging body that she would keep them there. If she looked at me, I would have either imploded like a shitty submarine or run out into oncoming traffic.

'Yeah, well, I don't know if this is a waste of time. I have kids – two kids – and they're so great. Two healthy girls who I love to death. I just feel a bit ...' I trailed off and looked at the closed door. It wasn't too late to fang it out of there.

'How old are your daughters?' she asked.

'Two and three,' I said. 'The eldest is almost four.' I cringed. I hated when people said that. Of course she was turning four – what other age would a three-year-old turn?

'Oh wow.' She raised her eyebrows. 'You're really in the thick of it, aren't you?'

'Yep, I guess so,' I gritted my teeth. When people said that, and they said it often, it inferred it was going to get easier, and for the life of me, I couldn't ever imagine it getting easier. I had made my bed, and I shall suffocate in it. I pushed on trying to explain why I was there. 'I just find myself quite annoyed a lot of the time. Is that normal?'

'Depends,' she said, now looking straight at me. I wished she would look away. 'How often are you annoyed, and what exactly does that look and feel like?'

I hated this. It was none of her business. I shouldn't have come. She could feel me pull back.

'Bronwyn, I'm going to ask you something and I hope you don't take offence.' Oh god. I needed to get out of there. 'Do you ...' She placed her hands on her lap and tilted her head, getting ready to observe my reaction to her dreaded question. 'Do you think you're a good mother?'

BANG. A SHOT WAS FIRED. I WAS HIT. MAN DOWN!

The Noise ramped up to a level so loud that I had to squint. I opened my mouth to reply, not knowing what I was even going to say, but instead of words, I just cried. My chin scrunched up and fat tears poured down my face and my hands unclenched as if I were surrendering. I let the words sink in and for the first time in four years I let myself buckle under the weight of it all. My brain ran through all my darkest memories of failure and desperation, and I forced myself to feel the sting of each of them, like lemon juice in a paper cut. I realised I wasn't expecting this question, but it was the most prominent and unspoken question that I circled around daily. Did I think I was a good mother? Of course I didn't. What kind of mother needs to exercise this much? What kind of mother cares about how they look this much? What kind of mother creates a completely separate life that runs parallel to the one she has with her children?

The doctor didn't move, she just let me sob heavily in her otherwise silent office until I could compose myself. I can't remember how long that took, but I imagine it took about as long as listening to a boring work colleague tell you about what they did on their weekend. Fucking ages. No one cares that you went to a farmers' market, Robert, organic produce can't make you interesting.

Finally, when the tears subsided, I looked at her, hoping she was playing Candy Crush on her phone, but she was just watching me blankly, as if this was the same show she had seen every single day of her life. What kind of sick fuck watches someone cry? I shouldn't call this excellent doctor a sick fuck but, honestly, I am pretty sure only serial killers watch grown-ups cry – look it up.

'It's okay, Bronwyn,' she said, pushing a box of tissues towards me. 'This feeling that you have is really normal. It's very clear to me that you're suffering from postnatal anxiety and it's more common than you think. The best part about it is it's really easy to treat. You don't have to live like this.'

Holy hell. She could fix this? I didn't have to feel like this anymore? The Noise would go away and I would ... enjoy my life? I wiped at my tears hastily, lied about definitely planning on seeing a psychologist (AS IF! I couldn't think of anything worse! Still can't, if I'm honest. Gross), took the script, paid the cranky receptionist and dashed to the pharmacy.

'You've taken this medication before?' the monotoned pharmacist asked.

'No,' I said proudly, as if my almost four years of suffering were a badge of honour. 'First time!'

I got home and gulped down the tablet with a glass of water. I'd briefly considered gin, but I felt like I should give the medication a fighting chance. The GP said it would take a few weeks to kick in, and the mad part of me scoffed at the whole thing being a waste of time, while the tiny hopeful part of me clung to the chance it was the beginning of something good. The beginning of The Noise shutting the fuck up. The beginning of coping with the chaos that came with this chapter of my life. The beginning of being a better mum.

Looking at myself in the mirror that night as I brushed my teeth, I let the GP's question run over me again. 'Do you think you're a good mother?' If I was honest with myself, I couldn't see past all my perceived mistakes to see anything good. I didn't think I was a good mother at that point. But maybe, I thought, in a few weeks, I would be.

If this chapter stings to read, or if you feel like you're on the cusp of imploding under the weight of negativity you've piled on yourself, go see a GP. Take it from someone who hates going to the GP more than that submarine guy hated being told 'I don't think this submarine is safe'. Go to the GP. You deserve happiness.

I'M NOT AS MAD AS YOU

The antidepressants took a couple of weeks to kick in. Each morning I'd look at my face in the bathroom mirror to see if I could notice any physical changes, but nothing. I still looked drained, the colour in my eyes, skin and hair still drab. I made a note to dye my hair that afternoon. That'd help, surely.

Even though the GP told me it takes a while to kick in, I still squeezed my eyes shut and hoped for a miracle. I have a long history of doing this – I don't believe in magic, relax, I'm not a witch, but when you're backed into a hopeless corner, you'll do anything to fight your way out of it. For my whole life I have squeezed my eyes shut, hoping whatever was happening wasn't actually happening, like when I stacked my BMX on the freshly poured bitumen in our cul-de-sac and ruined the outfit Nan had just bought me from Belconnen Grace Bros, or the time I waxed my moustache with wax so hot that it took all the skin off my upper lip, or when my nan died. I still squeeze my eyes shut, hoping she'll come back. I miss her endlessly. I thought the biggest tragedy of losing my nan was that I would never see her again, but now I know the biggest tragedy is that she never got to meet her great-grandchildren. She would have got such a kick out of them. Maybe once this medication set in, I too would get a kick out of them.

I squeezed my eyes shut. Please work, medicine. Hurry the fuck up and work.

After days of worrying the medicine wasn't strong enough, it finally started to kick in. I noticed my shoulders weren't creeping up towards my ears as the day went on, the rock on my chest wasn't as heavy and my teeth weren't constantly clenched. I no longer found slow walkers my mortal enemies and The Noise started to ease. It was still there, but I could now hear thoughts that weren't filled with self-hate, which was life-changing. I found myself *wanting* to go for walks to the park with the girls, to enjoy the September sun on my skin, rather than feeling like if I didn't get out of the house with them and storm furiously and aimlessly around Brunswick, I would perish.

The medicine was actually working and I was over the fucking moon!

I smiled at strangers and was happy to answer as many of the millions of questions the girls had about outer space and science. Obviously I made all of my answers up – I'm not a nerd – but an answer is an answer; just listen to a beauty pageant contestant when they give their solution to world peace – absolute horse shit, but we enjoy their ridiculous answers more than the real ones because it's performance art. I was LOVING life, and not because it was easy – I still had a two-year-old and a three-year-old, as well as an incredibly exhausting and thankless job as a teacher. Mark my words, I was still very much drowning, but I finally felt like I had a snorkel.

I could breathe. The medicine was working.

Walking to the park without a rock on my chest was incredible. I felt like that scene in *Muriel's Wedding* when Muriel walks down the aisle towards that blond swimmer who needs to marry her for a visa. I was completely and totally up myself and I imagined everyone was watching me float through the sun-drenched streets and thinking, 'How does she do it?'

Medicine, baby! The medicine was bloody working!

Arriving at Warr Park, the same park I had visited every single day for the past 250,000 years since becoming a mother, the yellow slide looked brighter, and the screech coming from the chains on the swing seemed to have dulled to a manageable squeak. Dare I say it, this park, which had been a main character in my downfall, looked ... pretty.

Holy flipping shit. The medicine was definitely working!

Another mother was there with her curly haired toddler and we shared a smile. She had a low ponytail tied back with a thick floral scrunchie, a loose-fitting denim dress and a filthy cardigan – a staple for all mothers with young kids. She had tired, kind eyes, and I was ready to become her best friend. Usually I avoided eye contact with people at the park because my anxiety nudged me into an unpredictable space, where I had no idea if I was going to either:

1. speak at them about utter nonsense like the IGA's latest refurb until they politely pulled their kid off the play equipment and made up an excuse as to why they had to leave, OR
2. be so hostile towards them that they would pull their kid off the play equipment and make up an excuse as to why they had to leave.

Either way, I was not a popular mum at any park, and I was finally ready to change that because ...

TA-DA! THE MEDICINE WAS WORKING!

'How old is he?' I asked, careful to keep my volume suited to a friendly chat with my new best friend rather than the machine gun that often replaced my mouth.

She smiled warmly at her son as he played with the tanbark. 'He's just turned two,' she said. 'How about your girls?'

Oh my god, we were getting along like a house on fire!

It was official: the medicine was *definitely* working!

'Olive is three and Edie is two,' I said proudly.

'Wow, two kids, and so close together. I don't know how you do it.'

'*Terribly*,' I thought, delivering a swift familiar punch to my guts.

Maybe the medicine wasn't working.

She noticed the smile leave my face, and she swooped in to fix whatever she'd accidentally broken. 'I mean, I think you're amazing. I don't think I could have another one! One is more than enough!' She giggled, keeping her eyes on her little boy. He was wearing denim overalls, the same shade as her dress. I wondered if she did that on purpose and, if so, did she match him or did he match her?

'I don't think I'm doing a great job,' I blurted out, surprising us both with my honesty. I thought this was going to be a lighthearted conversation about our dumb babies' sleep routines and favourite nursery rhymes, but here I was, picking at a scab that had hardly formed.

'You are,' she said. 'It might not feel like it, but you are.' We stood in silence as we watched the extensions of our hearts toddle around in front of us. I had heard countless people say that exact phrase to me, but there was something about the way she said that made it sound more believable.

'Maybe. I think it'll start to get better soon,' I said quietly, almost as a whisper. 'I … I went to the doctor recently for some help.' The air between us was heavy and cold, and I searched my brain as to why I would admit something so personal, so tender, to a complete stranger. Worse, to a woman who matched her outfits to her baby's, or vice versa.

'Which doctor?' she asked, now looking directly at me.

'Oh, I can't remember her name. I never go back to the same doctor if I can help it. I don't really trust any of them, if I'm honest.' I was being honest. Incredibly honest. More honest with this woman than I had been with most of my closest friends and family. What was happening?

Oh no. The medicine was not working.

She wrapped her filthy cardigan around her slim body, the way mums do when they're about to be frank. 'I hate them as well,' she admitted. She was back to looking at her son as he collected leaves from the big oak tree that shaded Warr Park. 'They poke you and prod you and tell you that it shouldn't feel the way it does.' She was becoming cryptic, but I still understood absolutely everything she was saying. 'They weigh your baby and check your nipples, and tell you that they're crying just as much as babies cry, which should feel like good news, but it isn't.'

I was too far in to back out now. 'Do you have a rock on your chest, too?' I asked.

'Oh yeah, all the time.' She smiled weakly. 'But it's getting lighter. The medication helps, but it's still definitely there – cold and unforgiving, right smack bam in the middle of your chest.'

We laughed, our shoulders slowly rising as if tiny weights were slipping off them.

'Did you get that insatiable fury like I did? Like, there's boiling hot sludge filling your body?' I felt like I was pushing my luck. Maybe this would be the part where she said she was actually a normal mum and she never felt insurmountable rage at anything whatsoever.

'Oh yeah,' she laughed. She was comfortable now; we both were. We leaned into our honesty and feasted on each other's. 'Once I yelled at a nurse for bringing me the wrong flavoured yoghurt!'

We laughed heartily.

'I didn't like the midwives at my last birth, but I don't think I yelled at them. I think I just wished they would fuck off.'

Still smiling, she said, 'Oh, mine wasn't a midwife, just a ... just a nurse.' She was pulling back slightly, but I hadn't really clocked it. I was too excited about finally finding someone who understood exactly where I had been for almost four long years. I wished I'd found her at the beginning, but here she was now, and I was absolutely beside myself with relief!

'Fuck nurses!' I yelled, intoxicated by the connection. 'And did you hear The Noise too?' I asked giddily.

'Yes.' Her tone had evened out. She was looking straight at me. 'You heard it too?'

'What? The Noise?' I laughed. 'Ah, yeah! Like all day, every day!' Finally I'd found someone else who could hear it.

'The voices, you mean?' Her smile had gone and she was searching my face for confirmation.

'Voices?' I mumbled. 'Not voices exactly, but the kettle and the cupboards and the crying all the time. Those noises. Is that what you heard?'

'Kind of. And voices.' She had turned her whole body towards me. 'It's a hard word to say, you know. No one warned me about it.'

'What word?' I asked. I suddenly found myself trying to hold on to my new-found connection as if I was climbing a rope covered in butter.

'The P word,' she said.

The P word? 'Postnatal anxiety?' I asked.

'No,' she said, looking at me quizzically. 'Psychosis.'

The Noise ramped up.

The medicine was definitely not working.

'Oh,' I whispered. 'I didn't have that.' I felt foolish that I had misunderstood our entire conversation. Her face flushed with embarrassment, and I wanted to give her a hug to make it go away, but I was frozen still. My mind ran swiftly over what her life might have looked like over the past two years. I looked down at her curly haired son and my heart bled for what he might have witnessed and what she remembers from what I am assuming was the most terrifying time of her life. The woman immediately sensed the shift in me, and pulled right back, sheepish. She'd revealed more than I had to offer and I wasn't prepared for it.

'I'm fine now,' she said firmly. 'I just had to go to hospital for a while. Ages actually. Don't worry, I'm fine now, I think ... Yeah, I think I'm fine.' Her smile was forced and I remained frozen, feet firmly in the tanbark, eyes directly on her, heart bleeding. I tried to find the words I would have wanted to hear if I was her, but I kept thinking of all the idiots who'd said dumb shit to me when I was at the peak of being mental, and I stayed silent. 'Anyway,' she said, 'we'd better go.' She rushed to her little boy and scooped him in her arms. 'My husband always worries if we're out for too long.'

I searched and searched my brain for the right thing to say, but I felt completely and utterly ill-equipped, so I said nothing. I just watched this woman, a total stranger, who was also my new best friend, walk into the late afternoon light with her squirmy son, the extension of her heart, the catalyst of her madness, in her arms.

I wrote this chapter last because it brings me so much shame. I had a woman standing in front of me sharing the hardest part of her life and I said nothing. I accidentally tricked her into a false sense of comfort with my musings of how my brain had betrayed me, and when she leaned in, I stepped back. It was like a trust fall gone wrong. I unwittingly let her feel like she was an absolute outcast in this motherhood game, and she probably fought harder than all of us to stay alive.

If I could go back in time to this moment I would. I'd say I am sorry that she experienced such a shitty time, when everything in the world had promised her that it would be pure magic. I'd say that motherhood sends even the strongest of us to the depths of madness and not all of us come back, but she did.

I hope that if this mother ever reads this book she knows that I think she is incredible – a queen among women – and that her baby boy is so unbelievably lucky that his mother, who was kissed on the forehead by madness, came back for him.

I left the park that day feeling like I was the luckiest woman in the world. For ages I'd thought that I had been incredibly unlucky to be burdened with The Noise, but that was fading, and the space around me was growing. This chance encounter with a healing mother showed me that I may have felt like I was being chased by the devil, but he never actually caught me.

I was going to be okay. Because the medicine was definitely working.

THIS TIME MIGHT JUST DESTROY ME

We were the first couple in our friendship group to have a baby – there is always one couple who goes first and all the other mates cheer on from the sidelines saying, 'A baby?! This is awesome! We're right behind you! We'll definitely have a baby too!' And then the baby is born and they all quietly decide to just get cavoodles. Fair play.

When Olive was born, everyone in our friendship group (including us) was like, 'Whaaaaat the hell is that?!' A baby was such a foreign concept until then, and Lukasz and I thought we were geniuses for being the first people in the world to make a baby. Then Edie came quickly after, which meant we had kids. PLURAL. Huge news. We'd broken some kind of record, surely, and we were convinced there would be an ABC *Australian Story* about us! We were so up ourselves about it that we would go to cafes and say, 'Table for four – two adults and, wait for it, TWO KIDS!' The waitstaff never visibly gave a shit, but we knew they were secretly impressed.

It goes without saying that having two babies at slightly different ages at the same time was exceptionally hard (I know, what a brave statement to make – it'll definitely be on my *Australian Story* episode, don't worry).

It was so difficult that we decided pretty early on that two kids was our absolute limit. Two kids was heaps. Two kids was enough. Many times I thought two kids was too many.

Then Covid happened, and Olive was six, and Edie was four (no longer difficult babies but ridiculously cute kids who could speak English and you could occasionally reason with), so we thought, 'Should we have just one more?' And I think that sentence uttered aloud got me pregnant.

It was 2020, so Melbourne was in the first year of lockdown and, because I was a teacher on long service leave, I was often lumped with a bunch of extra kids so my mates could work from home. If you are one of these mates and reading this right now, sorry if that sounds callous, but I literally don't know how to phrase it in a kinder way. I'm not cross, I would have done the exact same thing to you if I had a job and you didn't, but when morning sickness kicked in, looking after all those kids certainly made me feel like I drew the short straw. I felt like Nanny McPhee if she was shit at her job.

The day I found out I was pregnant with Ari, my third and final baby, is still so clear in my mind. I knew I was pregnant before I'd even done the test. No, this isn't because I am one of those women with super-feminine instincts who can tell when her period is coming by looking at the moon or whether her unborn baby is a boy or a girl by the direction of the wind. As you've probably picked up, I hate learning, which includes anything about my own body. I am too lazy to research why, what and when something is happening to me because if it's going to happen, why fight it?

I'm not a naturally curious person. I have an illogical fear that I only have enough brain space for a certain number of skills and facts, and mine is currently jam-packed with skills I use frequently. I worry that if someone teaches me a new one, a skill I use daily will fall out the back of my head, and I am simply not willing to risk the lyrics to TLC's 'No Scrubs' for something like sudoku or CPR, no thanks!

I thought my curiosity would kick in when I left school and wasn't forced to learn things anymore, but no. I thought that when I finished uni I would start to *want* to learn things, but nah. I thought that when I became pregnant with my first baby I would want to learn about what was happening to my body but, NOPE, my brain was like, 'Righto, you're going to get bigger for a bit,' and, honestly, that was enough information for me.

I downloaded a pregnancy app – I'm not a psycho. I only downloaded it for one reason, though, and that was so I could see the baby's size each week. The app tells you the size of the baby and compares it to something you can understand – one week it's the size of a poppyseed, the next it's the size of a blueberry, and eventually it's the size of a gigantic financial burden. The tracking helps.

The antenatal appointments for the girls' pregnancies were a waste of my time. Ari's pregnancy was a completely different kettle of fish, but I'll get to that bin fire in good time. I found the appointments with the midwives a waste of everyone's time, especially mine. The bubbly midwife would ask, 'Any questions this week, Bron?' And I would think, 'Just the same one I have every week: why are you so obsessed with me?'

My lack of curiosity wasn't an issue in my relationship with Lukasz until pregnancy. He is a naturally curious person – he is obsessed with geography and history, which are two mandatory subjects I weaselled my way out of in high school because I told the Year 10 coordinator that Mum was too busy to cook dinner for us kids anymore so it had become my job, which at this point wasn't completely untrue. I cooked a lot of pasta bake for my siblings when I was in high school, a dish laced with grim memories for me, which is annoying because it's so damn easy. I pitched myself as a regular Cinderella who had no time for geography or history, and the sucker bought it. He was a PE teacher, though, so I think those subjects didn't spark much joy for him either.

Lukasz became frustrated that I didn't ask the midwife questions during Olive's antenatal appointments, so I suggested he come along and ask whatever he wanted to ask. He planned to take the morning off work for the next appointment. What's his job? I don't know. I've been with this man since 2012 and we have three children together – it is TOO LATE FOR ME TO ASK NOW. I'm just waiting for one of our kids to be interested in him enough to say, 'Oh, Dad, what do you do?' And I'll roll my eyes at them like, *How do you not know?* as I listen hungrily to his answer.

He came along to the appointment and the midwife looked around the waiting room and said, 'Bron? Oh, and Daddy!' Gross. Why do midwives have to make everything weird? Normally, if you don't know someone's name you just ask them, but not midwives. Daddy? Yuck! Flirty much? We went into the examination room and she asked me if I had any questions. I said, 'No, but you'll never believe your luck ... because this guy' – I point at Lukasz – 'has heaps.' So this midwife saw not only a present father but an *interested* one and she almost slid off her chair.

I got comfy in my chair, thinking we would be there for hours. I was fully prepared to zone the hell out until Lukasz asked, 'What's the record?'

The midwife furrowed her brow and said, 'The record? Of what?'

'Of babies.'

I thought, 'Oh, this is going to be *gooood*.'

The midwife spoke under her breath as if she was trying to solve a riddle. 'The record of babies? What is the record of … babies?' Then she looked straight at Lukasz and said, 'I'm sorry, I'm not following.'

He shifted in his chair and said slowly, 'What is the record of babies *born*?'

By this stage she was looking at me with the expression *Is there something wrong with him?* I gave her nothing because I was having the time of my life. 'Sorry, Lukasz,' she said sheepishly, 'I'm not sure what you're trying to ask.'

He looked bewildered, as if he was asking the easiest question in the world and she was acting like an idiot. He spoke even slower: 'What is the record of babies born in a day in this hospital?'

The midwife gave a heavy sigh of relief. Finally she understood his question. 'Ohhhh,' she said, giggling. Then her eyes narrowed, her smile disappeared and she shook her head. 'I don't know.'

And THAT WAS HIS ONLY QUESTION! That was IT! After ALL OF THAT, that WAS ALL HE WANTED TO KNOW! I couldn't believe it!

We left the examination room: the midwife was disappointed, Lukasz was sheepish and I was smug as shit. He didn't come to any more appointments for the next seven years after that.

Anyway, the reason I knew I was pregnant with Ari was that mentally I was fading. The muscles in my face felt slack, sounds and colours were dulled and I felt like I was being slowly erased. I went for a walk with the kids and felt absolutely nothing. No joy at their laughter, no frustration at their nagging, nothing. I felt that familiar feeling of nothingness, and it kicked me in the guts. I was pregnant. I just knew it. Oh, fuck.

I continued on the walk and cried behind my sunglasses because, even though we wanted this baby, I knew I was going to lose myself again. I knew that all the mess I'd made, which had taken me years to clean up, was about to burst into my life again and this time it might just destroy me.

I felt so close to the flames when the girls were tiny, so what the hell was I thinking, traipsing on down the newborn path again? Surely this time I wouldn't be so lucky as to emerge in one piece? I was going to write 'unscathed' there, but I didn't emerge unscathed the first times. I emerged from my postnatal-anxiety hellscape scathed as hell. As soon as I was medicated, I looked like Sarah Connor from *Terminator*, if she'd been hit by a car and vomited on.

Awful memories of helplessness came at me like a tidal wave and I returned to the familiar stage of 'fight or flight'. I was at Merri Creek with my kids and my mates' kids, so I couldn't really do either unless a jogger came around the corner and wanted to punch on with me. Now that I think about it, if I got into a fight in public, fewer people would drop their kids at my house. What a missed opportunity.

I got home from the walk and Lukasz was there in his tracksuit. God, that man really embraced the tracksuit during Covid and, lemme tell ya, he didn't let it go. He has more tracksuits than *Little Britain*'s Vicky Pollard and, since 2020, he has unashamedly donned one daily. Lukasz would, of course, deny this, but it is widely known that this is his clothing of choice because one day I was chatting with another mum at the school gate and I said, 'Lukasz is in Europe at the moment,' to which she replied,

'Will he only be wearing tracksuits over there as well?'

Lukasz saw me slumped at the kitchen bench and he asked me if I was okay, and I said, 'I need a pregnancy test.' His face lit up, which was a good sign, but it only highlighted just how differently we experienced this early stage of life.

'Already?! Wow! We only tried once!' He beamed with virile pride, which grossed me out to no end. I hate how blokes feel like they can take any credit for any part of a pregnancy or birth. I don't give a shit about science, the pregnancy and birth are ALL thanks to the woman. All my pregnancies and all my births were me and me alone. Lukasz did nothing and, no, this isn't me saying he was a bad partner during these times, he was wonderful (except for Ari's birth, but I'll get to that in due course), but there is literally nothing he could ever have done to take anywhere near half the weight of the pregnancies or half the pain of the births.

As he puffed his chest out in his grubby hoodie at the news of another baby, I could have thrown my phone at him. I should have been the proud one! I not only *did this*, but I was *doing this.* I feel cross remembering his reaction but, if I'm honest, all my feelings paled in stark contrast to the terror I was feeling. I burst into tears and his excitement shifted to bewilderment.

'What's wrong?' he asked.

'I don't know if I can do this again,' I sobbed.

'But I thought you said you wanted another baby?'

'I did, but what happens if ... I go mad again?'

Saying the words aloud was one of the scariest things I'd ever done, and I'd bungee-jumped off a crane at Surfers Paradise when I was nineteen. I was petrified, as if merely saying the words would breathe life back into the beast that had tormented me for the most precious years of my daughters' lives. But I was also terrified of how Lukasz would respond. This was the man who trusted me with our babies. The man who was supposed to think I was incredible. The man who wore tracksuits for every occasion!

He wrapped his arms around me and said, 'You won't! But if you did, we know how to fix it. We'll see the red flags and we'll be on top of it quick smart!'

I softened because I believed him. Surely the one silver lining of going mad was the ability to spot it early the next time it crept up on you. I knew what madness felt like so, as with a cold sore, I would recognise the tingle and act swiftly so it didn't get so bad I'd piss the bed (maybe that's a personal symptom, but you get the gist).

I let Lukasz hold me for a while while I sobbed heavily into his hoodie. Not from fear this time, but relief. The numbness subsided, and I let the relief wash over me. Thank fuck. Thank fucking fuck.

This was actually amazing! I was having a baby and there was a chance I wasn't going to drown in anxiety. I was having a baby and there was a chance I wouldn't hate the experience. I was having a baby and, because I knew the early signs, I was not going to go mad.

If only I knew then that I had only experienced one flavour of postnatal madness. If only I knew then I had no idea just how grim it could get.

WIND BENEATH MY WINGS

'Bron, come look at what Lukasz did! He put on a load of washing! Bronnie, come have a look! Gosh, he's a good man! Your father wouldn't know how to even turn the washing machine on!'

Mum, like most women of her generation, thinks that the blokes in my generation are incredible when they do the bare fucking minimum, and it absolutely kills me.

'You and your sisters are so lucky. Those men are angels,' she'd gush.

'Why?' my sisters and I would ask.

'Because they help at Christmas!'

Fucking hell, Helen, he put on a load of washing. Who cares? And it isn't just Hels: a lot of women from Mum's generation, and even more from the generation who came before, are positively amazed when they see a bloke doing a lick of domestic labour or hands-on parenting. The blokes from those generations mustn't have done a bloody thing and, as far as I can tell, they didn't. Mum has always had a soft spot for Lukasz and she'll be the first person to sing his praises when given the opportunity. Every single time she visits, this is what will happen:

Helen opens the front door: 'Hello?'

Kids run down the hallway: 'Mama Hels!'

Helen hugs them hungrily: 'HELLO, MY DARLINGS!'

Me walking down the hallway: 'Hi Mum!'

Helen looks up and smiles: 'Hi dar—'

Lukasz pushes past me: 'MAMA HELS!'

Helen throws the kids to the floor and wraps her arms around Lukasz: 'OH, HELLO, MY DARLING BOY!'

I get it, Mum, he's a good bloke. I don't know why you seem surprised I didn't end up with a dud, but I won't look too far into that. Don't get me wrong, I love that they love each other. I imagine it would be heartbreaking to choose a partner and find out that they clash with one of your main characters. But Lukasz and Mum are two naughty little kids together – they sit up late out the back, drink wine and smoke ciggies until they've both run out. Mum tells him the same stories over and over, and Lukasz laughs his head off every single time, as if it's the first time he's heard them. At the start I thought he was doing it to be polite, but he says he genuinely loves listening to her stories, so I guess it's like Nan telling us the same stories all the time: we loved them not for the content, but for how she came to life telling them. I guess Hels is Lukasz's answer to Nan. I'm sure she'll love reading that.

I should also mention here that Mum isn't wrong to think Lukasz is a phenomenal man: he genuinely is. When I was a teacher, a job that was harder than buttering soft bread with a steak knife, I was only 'working' three days (well, I should say I was only getting paid for three days – all the extra work was out of the kindness of my heart and maybe the industry's expectation to get a million things done in a short amount of time and then be grateful/apologetic about the school holidays, when teachers just fall in a heap and try to rebuild in time for the next term) and Lukasz worked full-time. This meant that I was in charge of most of the cleaning, all of the cooking, shopping, bathtimes et cetera. I was always, always there for bedtime, and while Lukasz was home from work to help, little kids tend to only want their mums at bedtime (poor Lukasz), so I would have to do them too. Why did I go mad again? Hard to pinpoint what exactly sent me over the edge, but if I had to guess, it was the crushing weight of it all. So good!

Since leaving teaching, I worked nights and had to travel interstate quite a bit as a stand-up comedian. Obviously this drastic career shift made a whopping change to our family life. Lukasz started doing the shopping, loads of the bedtimes and now does all the cooking (thank Christ: I genuinely hate cooking so much, holy hell, if I never have to cook anything ever again in my life I would be so fucking happy – sorry for swearing so much, I'm just really bloody passionate about that). It is worth mentioning he never complains about any of it, which is wild to me because complaining about the shit bits is actually one of my favourite things to do: opportunity missed, mate!

In 2019, I was in my final year of teaching. I didn't know it was my final year of teaching at the time, but I am beyond glad it was because it was starting to suffocate me. I had been medicated for a little over a year by then and, while I still very much felt the rock on my chest and The Noise crept in on vulnerable days, it all felt pretty manageable. I'd quit CrossFit, so I found myself face to face with the ruins my anxiety had created. Incredibly, I still had everyone who mattered to me: Claire, my siblings, Hels, a smattering of close friends, Lukasz and the kids. I thought I had taken a chainsaw to my life and identity in a dramatic attempt at surviving The Noise, and there were definitely some casualties and debris, but everyone who truly meant something to me was waiting in the wings for my return. The most patient of all was Lukasz.

The relief of finding my feet again was intoxicating. I couldn't believe my luck that after the hurricane of postnatal anxiety, the best bits remained! Surely it would all be smooth sailing now? SURELY! But now that I had the capacity to breathe and sit still, there was enough space to think about the rest of my life. Did I want to teach for the rest of it? Hard no. Every year, the workload seemed to get bigger, the colleagues became more hateful and the kids told teachers to 'get fucked' more. It was a sinking ship, and I felt like I had *just* survived one of those, so I needed a lifeboat out of there.

Given how much I hate learning, leaving the only job I was qualified for seemed a bit mental. I overheard a colleague telling someone she'd gone to see a psychic to see if her unborn baby was a boy or a girl (seems like there was an easier way to get that answer, but whatever), and I thought, 'Stuff it, I'll see if a psychic knows what I should be doing.'

I don't believe in magic, I just was desperate to see if anyone had an answer to my predicament. I needed a way out of teaching because last time I'd felt trapped, I almost blew up my entire life and everyone else in it. Yep, when the consequence is that high, a psychic was worth a try!

I arrived at her second-storey flat on the other side of town and immediately wanted to leave. The music was wispy and the incense was so strong that it filled my nostrils like hot cement. This was not my vibe and I felt embarrassed to be there. Before I had the chance to bolt, a woman named Jade, my psychic, bowed in front of me and then ushered me into an even more more woo-woo room where I would bite my tongue and swallow my sceptical outbursts for an entire hour.

Jade was breathtakingly beautiful, with long, flowing dark hair, tanned skin decorated with intricate and cryptic tattoos, and piercing blue eyes. I figured someone this stunning could say anything and tired losers like me would believe it. She sat me at a tiny table covered in crystals that Olive and Edie would have loved. She asked me to relax, but this was as relaxed as I was ever going to be in a place this jarring. I felt like I was overdressed, even though I was wearing skinny-leg jeans and a tucked-in T-shirt, and as I watched her move crystals around, I wished my short hair was as long as hers. I wished anything of mine was like hers, especially my ability to believe in pretty rocks. The only rock I had any experience with was the one that rested on my chest.

When the session kicked off, Jade kept trying to clear her throat, which was pretty annoying. I wished she would just get a glass of water, but she remained seated opposite me and said, 'Oh my goodness, there is something in your throat.'

Okay, there it is, she's mental. No, Jade, there is something in *your* throat. I knew this would be a waste of time.

'No,' I said, 'I'm fine. Did you need water?'

'No, there is something in your throat chakra.'

Okay, I had heard enough. Jade went in too hard too quickly, so I was ready to leave.

She continued. 'Are you a singer?'

I tried not to scoff at this beautiful idiot. 'No, Jade. I'm definitely not a singer.'

'Oh,' she said, 'because there is something in your throat chakra that needs to come out.'

'I'm a teacher, Jade. I speak all day. Could that be it?' I was being nice. I regretted coming.

'Maybe,' she said unconvinced. 'Let's keep going.'

Whatever Jade went on to say I didn't hear. I chalked this up as a waste of time and used the rest of the hour making mental notes about what I needed to do for the rest of the day. Jade cleared her throat intermittently throughout her waffling and, by the end of the session, I just wanted to pay and leave. Before I got up, she grabbed both of my hands in hers. I became immediately self-conscious about how cold and rough my hands were compared to her soft, warm hands.

'There *is* something in your throat you need to explore,' she said, staring into my eyes. 'You need to be using your voice for something else. That's the strongest message that has come through for me today, and I hope you're open to listening to it.'

'Right, definitely, yep,' I said, pulling my hands back to my lap. 'I'll sort that out for sure!' I tried not to sound disingenuous, but it was a losing game. There wasn't a tiny bit of me that thought Jade was right in the head, so in fear of saying anything too honestly, I paid and rushed towards my car as quickly as I could.

The long drive home was frustrating: I'd worked out that I'd wasted most of my day and half a tank of petrol to watch a pretty woman cough for an hour. It wasn't until I got to the last set of traffic lights before my house that a penny dropped (or a crystal – I don't know how these things work, I'm not a witch). I grabbed my phone and texted my friend Doris, who shared an office with me at work. Doris is the wisest and most maternal woman I've ever met, and she always treated me like I was made for something more than teaching. When I was losing my marbles, she was so gentle with me, and I know she would have had my back when everyone else was questioning if I was properly mental.

Doris is one of the greatest mates I've ever had, and not just because she is fiercely loyal, but because she pumped my tyres up when I was flat as a tack. One way she pulled me out of a dark mood was asking enough questions that I inevitably told a long-winded story and transformed from a husk of a woman to a performer, and she would transform from the busy office lady to the best audience anyone has ever had. She would swing her wheelie chair around, give me her undivided attention, slap her thighs and roar laughing the whole way through. She was the first person to say to me, 'I think you would be a brilliant stand-up comedian, Bron!' And she would say it often. I don't know if I would have ever tried comedy without her years of encouragement. The world doesn't deserve her.

At the traffic lights I messaged her: *Should I actually try stand-up comedy?*

And before I could even put the phone down, she replied, *YES!*

That night I asked Lukasz to have a few drinks with me to 'reconnect', but it was mostly for me to get enough courage to float this idea by him. I felt vulnerable beyond belief, and I wasn't sure I had won back his trust in my decision-making skills since losing the plot. But I needed him on board. If he wasn't, there was no point in trying.

'What would you say if I said I wanted to try stand-up comedy?' I asked, staring into my wine glass, fearful that he would laugh at the idea.

'Stand-up comedy? You would be brilliant at it, Bron!' He was smiling so hard that his face almost split wide open. And that's all I needed – his blessing to chase a dream I didn't even know I was hiding.

That was June 2019, and I taught my last-ever class that December.

As a family we took a massive risk to go from two incomes to one, and it hasn't always been easy. Some would say I replaced my CrossFit obsession with a comedy obsession, and there were chapters where they would have been correct, but comedy makes so much sense to me, and it never splits the skin on my hands or breaks my spine in half. Comedy is wildly demanding and mentally consuming, so if I am home, I am often thinking about it, but I'm a better mum because of it. I can finally say I love my job, and without Lukasz's unwavering support, there is no way I could have achieved this.

I can't tell you how many bedtimes I've missed because of comedy, and there is a part of me, the self-flagellating part, that is convinced I will regret that, but the logical part knows I have to do comedy to be the mum I wanted to be. I was never going to be the stay-at-home mother, or the mum who makes homemade granola slices for the kids' lunchboxes. My mother showed no interest in those things, and I can appreciate why. I would feel so trapped if motherhood was the only thing that gave me purpose, because what happens when they grow up and move out? Do I just die? I am showing my kids what it means for me to be happy, and that is to do a job I love, as well as be their mother. I know I am a better mother to them since leaving teaching because I am happy now, and I couldn't have arrived at this privileged place of contentment without Lukasz.

My mother is correct in thinking Lukasz is a phenomenal man. He is so kind and patient with all of us, but especially me. He has seen so many different sides of me, sides I am proud of and sides I never want to see again, and he has loved me fiercely through every phase. I don't know how he does it.

ARI'S LABOUR

During my pregnancy with Ari, we decided to move from Melbourne to Brisbane to be closer to Lukasz's tight-knit family and further away from Victoria's harsh Covid restrictions. I loved Melbourne, but the thought of having a baby where it was warm and we'd be doted over by family was too good to pass up, so for two years we lived a Queensland life and it was glorious. It was the place my comedy career truly started, and the place my beautiful baby boy was born. I was excited for my kids to grow up with their Polish grandparents where their babcia would cook more food for them than they could eat and their dziadek would take them to the park when we were too tired to. They would have a long list of warm and invested ciocias, wujeks, aunties, uncles and cousins to connect with and I would immerse myself in his wholesome family and be the best daughter-in-law anyone had ever seen. I don't know if I'll ever win that last award, and we only stayed in Brisbane for two years, but I will always look fondly on that time with Lukasz's beautiful family who truly welcomed this foul-mouthed woman into their lives.

Thanks to Ari's enormous head, he was induced two weeks early. I absolutely hate pregnancy, so this was very welcome news to me. I joked with the midwife at the thirty-week check-up that I was ready for him to be born then, and she gave me a five-minute TED Talk on why it wasn't safe to induce me that early. I was too annoyed by her earnestness to tell her I was joking, so I zoned out and let her rabbit on about what I should and shouldn't be doing.

I find midwives and GPs the same – mostly patronising and dismissive, apart from a few who can save your life with a smile. I was hoping the midwife for Ari's birth would be a salt-of-the-earth kind of woman who had given birth a million times herself. I know it's unfair, but I find it hard to trust midwives who have never had a baby. It kind of feels like trusting a mechanic who rides a bicycle, or a plumber who shits in a plastic bag. I also felt safer with older women, whether they'd had babies or not – they had experienced life as a woman for decades and having that wisdom in the room with me felt non-negotiable. For Edie's birth I had two midwives: a qualified one and a midwife in training. I couldn't tell which was which because they both looked fifteen, which was absolutely infuriating because it felt like two of my Year 9 students were in the birthing suite telling me what to do, as one of them narrated the birth to the other.

'Okay, cool, what you can see her doing now is she's moving a bit ... weirdly' – giggle – 'which *could* mean she's getting ready to transition into Stage Two, which is what?'

'Fetal expulsion: she needs to push.'

'Yass queen, that's right! Oh, wait, false alarm, she was just moving herself so she could flip us off. Stand down.'

I couldn't fucking stand those youthful bitches. I really needed a Marg or a Sherryn or a Barbara with me for Ari's birth because, from what they were all saying, it was going to be a tough one. It was also going to be my last one, so I did yearn for it to be as magical as the hippies said it could be. As I have mentioned many times, I don't believe in magic, but I do love the idea of feeling powerful during a horrific physical experience such as childbirth.

I spent the entire pregnancy with Ari hoping to achieve a lovely birth. As my belly grew bigger and bigger, I would tell myself that I was in control of his birth. It was my body and I was going to be a goddess of strength and femininity when I brought him into this world. All I needed was exactly the right people with me.

Narrator: 'She did not have the right people with her.'

The night before I was induced, Lukasz and I put our two little girls to bed, cherishing the last night we would be a family of four. Olive and Edie were seven and five, and they were champing at the bit to meet their baby brother. I wasn't scared of labour; there were too many things to look forward to to get bogged down in how much it was going to hurt. Like, watching my girls meet him, or just kissing his tiny hands for the first time. I was also quietly confident that this birth was going to be the most transformative experience of my life. I thought that my perceived failings as a mother so far – the anxiety, the avoidance, the rushing – would all be washed away as I met this birth head-on and proved to myself that I was capable of remarkable things.

I closed the door to the girls' room and walked into the kitchen, where Lukasz stood with his phone in his hand. It was a balmy autumn night in our Brisbane home and I was both exhausted and excited. I was just about to ask him what show we should watch on the telly when he decided to let me know that, after almost nine years together, he was still full of surprises.

'Because we're having a baby tomorrow, is it alright if I invite two of my mates over to have a last hoorah?'

What? I was stunned. He took my silence as a 'Go for it!' and, before I knew it, his two mates were drinking with him on the back deck. To give you an understanding of what kind of night this was, I'll just give you the nicknames of these mates: Walshy and Donga. They got stuck into this last hoorah and I went to bed only to hear Mum's taxi pull into the driveway. Helen was here.

She was thrilled to find these young scallywags smashing booze on the back deck and, as a seasoned drinker herself, she jumped straight in with them. We lived in an old Queenslander where you could hear absolutely everything. If someone farted down the opposite end of the house, you'd seriously wonder if you'd done it. So I listened to them booze on, which wouldn't usually have been a big deal, but I was so terrified of being too tired to be the powerful goddess I'd promised myself I'd be that I lay in bed and seethed.

In the morning, I woke and looked over at Lukasz, who was very hungover. You know when someone is so hungover, their features move? He looked nothing like him – his phone wouldn't even register Face ID. I had no time to berate him for this because I had to walk to the hospital, so I told him to wash his face and get on with it. We lived in the same suburb as the hospital, so the walk wasn't long and it was always our plan to walk there, but it brings me so much joy to tell people Lukasz was so hungover that I had to walk myself to the hospital. He never corrects me either; he knows it's the least he can give me.

When we arrived at the hospital, our midwife was older than me, which, at first glance, was a huge green flag. However, it didn't take long to work out she was from the generation that thought men who did the bare minimum were incredible, which was a huge red flag. A big old flaming red flag covered in blood, fire and side-eyes.

She looked at Lukasz and smiled. 'You came!'

The red flag was enormous by this stage. Her admiration of Lukasz for just showing up meant this labour was going to be properly fucked. I did a quick mental calculation: I had a midwife who was more impressed with Lukasz's presence than anything I could ever do, and a man who was so hungover he was sweating rum and Cokes. This birth was really going to be a solo effort, and I was already exhausted.

The labour kicked off and it was excruciating – far worse than Olive's birth or Edie's. I quickly realised that all the tricks I had read about online were useless. I tried to imagine my body was a red balloon, and with each contraction it would grow larger. I tried to picture the baby coming down the birth canal instead of focusing on the pain. I tried to focus on my breathing as a distraction, but nothing worked. I was in agony.

I was freezing, too, which I expected. I don't know why they make birthing suites so icy cold. They must be like, 'Oh, she's not uncomfortable enough!' So, in between horrific, body-contorting contractions, I waddled to my maternity bag and pulled out my white woollen shawl with flowers embroidered on it and tassels around the bottom. I sighed as I wrapped my sore, swollen body in the shawl and looked up at Lukasz, who was standing there, shivering, in a T-shirt, shorts and thongs.

'Did you ...' he was struggling to find the right words. 'Did you pack one for me?'

Wrong words.

'Did I pack you a maternity bag?!' I was flabbergasted. I looked at the midwife, who thought he was the duck's nuts, and thought, 'Surely she'll be on my side now!', but she wasn't.

'Oh, let him have it,' she said impatiently. 'I have blankets for you.' She walked over to a cupboard, pulled out two scratchy public-hospital blankets, and unwrapped my woollen shawl from my sore, swollen body and handed it to Lukasz, who in turn wrapped his shivering man body in it, then lay down on the plastic couch designed for labouring women and went to sleep.

And she encouraged him to act like this. In the hours leading up to his snooze, she would say, 'You must be so tired, Lukasz. No point in you both being awake, I'll look after her.' And when he did drift off, she left the room as if her job was done.

When she was back, tapping away at a hospital computer, I wanted to ask her for any advice she had, but I couldn't find the strength to talk. I must have been too noisy for Lukasz, because at one point he stirred from his slumber to offer me some advice: 'No pain, no gain.' My eyes shot over to the midwife. SURELY she'd be on my side now!

'He's right,' she said, without even turning to face me.

I was livid and so lonely. Five hours passed and my physical and mental strength were fading. I could feel Ari's head literally moving my bones – my pelvis widening and my hips aching. Pure agony. I needed an epidural, and I began the begging process. The largely absent midwife clicked on her computer and said, 'We will see what we can do. A lot of women are in today – it's a popular day to be born!' She smiled in Lukasz's direction, awaiting his approval of her shit joke, and he obliged. What a team!

I wept as another contraction started rolling in, and said, 'I can't do this anymore.' She put her hand on my shoulder and said sternly, 'Pull yourself together!' And then walked back out of the room. Was I being that difficult? I had no fight left in me to argue with her, so I worked on being silent.

For hours I waited for the anaesthetist. I can't remember how long because I wasn't watching the clock, but if I had to guess, it would have been roughly 450 hours. The labour was excruciating. It was one minute of blindingly white pain that started in my womb and spread to the top of my head and the tips of my toes. Then I would have a forty-second rest, when I tried to sleep, and then the contraction would start again. Hours. I weakly begged the apathetic midwife to go find him, and when I tried to wake Lukasz, she said, 'Oh, leave him, he's so tired.'

Finally, a tall ginger doctor walked in. He wore bright blue scrubs and a cartoon-themed cap. He looked around the room and sighed heavily, as if my request that he do his job was the biggest inconvenience he'd ever faced in his life. I didn't have the strength or the time to worry about how he was feeling, so I unleashed.

'Thank Christ you're here! You have to hurry, I need that epidural now. Don't worry about going over the risks, I've had one before, I just need it now!' I was on my side, clutching at the bedsheets. I'm not sure if anyone has ever looked so desperate.

He looked at the midwife and raised his eyebrows. She shrugged and gave him a knowing smile. They were talking about me without words, and if I wasn't being torn in half I would have addressed it. 'I can't talk to her like this, she's hysterical,' he said to the midwife.

She nodded. 'Yeah, she's been pretty difficult.'

I was outnumbered. I needed that epidural so badly, so I didn't argue. I made myself silent as he listed all the potential risks of the epidural in a monotone while he studied his fingernails. I wanted to say to him, 'Hurry the fuck up, you fuckhead. I have been labouring for seven hours with a fucking bitch and a bloke I will never fuck again. Please, for the love of god, do your fucking job and put a fucking needle in my fucking spine,' but I didn't. I knew it would prolong everything, so I bit my tongue and let him reel off noises that sounded like words. Once he was finished, he said, 'Right, slide over to the edge of the bed. Lukasz, we might need you to hold Bron's legs for this.'

The midwife blurted out, 'Oh, he's pretty tired.' We all looked over at Lukasz, who was still lying on the plastic labouring couch wrapped in my woollen shawl.

'I can help,' he said, slowly lifting himself off the couch.

'Oh, you're a good man, Lukasz!' The midwife gushed. I hated everything about that woman.

'Just one more contraction, Bron,' the doctor said. 'And when that's done, I'll insert the needle into your spine.' One more contraction. I could do one more. If he asked me to do two, I would have chosen death. I clenched my eyes shut, gritted my teeth and let the familiar wave of agony take over my entire body. Once it was finished, I kept my eyes shut and said helplessly, 'It's done, do it now. Please.'

The midwife piped up with a sentence no one was expecting. 'Wait, doctor, don't put the needle in yet! Lukasz? Lukasz, wake up.'

My excruciating and unforgiving contraction had gone for so long that Lukasz had fallen asleep on my lap. I shook my legs and the midwife gently tapped his back. When he finally came to, and the nurse had made sure he was okay, the doctor said, 'Well, we missed our window. One more contraction, Bron, and I'll give you the needle. Are you okay, Lukasz?'

I couldn't believe it. I had promised myself I only needed to endure one more, but once again I had been betrayed by every single moron in the room. One. More. Contraction.

Contractions, by the way, feel like someone is pushing their entire arm up your arsehole and squeezing your organs and, just before they explode, they slowly release them.

One more of those? Yeah, sure, no worries.

Finally, after one million years of labour and one epidural, I could sleep. I was allowed to sleep for a whole hour before that bitch midwife shook me awake and said, 'It's go time!' I peeled open my eyes just in time to see two new, incredibly young midwives walk into the room. 'Bron, this is Georgia and Lauren. They'll deliver your baby, my shift is OVER!' She sang the last word in Georgia's and Lauren's faces.

Georgia and Lauren. No. Those are not the names of the midwives I needed. I just really needed one and, like I said, she needed to be called Marg or Sherryn or Barbara. These midwives were so young, but I was too tired and disappointed to ask for a different one. I lay there, barely awake, as Lukasz's biggest fan talked about me like I wasn't in the room. 'Obs are fine, but she hasn't coped well with the pain. She's had an epidural, which was, shall I say, 'dramatic'!' All three of them laughed and I felt nothing. No rage anymore, no pain, just emptiness. I wanted to sleep.

Georgia and Lauren looked over my charts and talked about Ari's giant head. 'Oh, the baby has macrocephaly. This could be a tricky one!' I didn't feel like I was even in the room, and they were talking about me like I wasn't. I didn't care anymore. 'Bron?' Georgia was talking to me like I was a lost demented woman. 'Bron, you're going to have to sit up and push now. Baby is ready to come out.'

I was completely drained. Push? How? I was a bag of flesh and I needed to sleep.

'Come on, babe. You can do it.' Lukasz was standing next to my bed and holding my hand. My shawl was in a heap on the plastic couch, so I assumed he was ready to start helping now. I nodded slowly and let them tinker around under the sheet. My body did not belong to me. Maybe it never had.

A new midwife walked in, this one older, with sensible shoes and great big bosoms. She looked at my chart and walked over to the end of the bed without saying a word. I didn't care who was down there at this point. Lauren picked up some gigantic scissors and held them above my knees. She snapped them open and shut a few times, demonstrating the sharp, slicing sound of the metal. What the fuck? 'We're just going to give you an episiotomy, Bron. Baby's head is too big to come out without it.'

'He's a boy,' I kept thinking. '*His* head. Say that.'

The older midwife took the scissors from Lauren's hands and said firmly, 'Let's just see what Bron can do first. Her body was made for this, let's give her a chance to push him out by herself.'

There she was. My Marg/Sherryn/Barbara. Thank fucking fuck.

'Righto, Bron, and push!' Marg/Sherryn/Barbara said. I put my chin to my chest and pushed like my life depended on it. I shut my eyes and pictured all the people who had poked, prodded and patronised me since coming through those doors and I pushed my son out.

'There you go, girls!' Marg/Sherryn/Barbara laughed. 'That's how you push a baby out!'

She pulled him up and put him on my chest. He was perfect and he was all mine. Lukasz burst into tears and kissed my head over and over and over. 'You're amazing, Bron,' he blubbered.

'That she is,' said Marg/Sherryn/Barbara firmly. 'That she is.'

Needless to say, that was not how I wanted my final birth to go. I needed someone with me. I wanted Lukasz there, and I needed someone who knew me to just be there with me. Because it was during Covid, labouring women could only have one support person, which was was, simply put, cooked. Usually Lukasz was excellent in a crisis – in only a few days' time he would prove this over and over – but for that night, while my body split open and took on a life of its own, I needed more people. I needed my sister. Amy would have been the perfect person to have with me: she would have held my hand and silently mouthed, 'YOU NEED TO FUCK OFF' to the awful midwife. So many of us were robbed of the birth we deserved during Covid. Labour is a lonely experience that can be a little less lonely with the right people there, and I for one really needed my big brother and my big sister with me. Hamish and Amy were exactly who should have been there – one to hold my hand and the other to shake Lukasz awake by saying, 'Wake up, Poland!! You can sleep when you're dead!'

We keep finding new ways to tell women that their bodies don't belong to them, and, incredibly, childbirth is right at the top of the list. I feel for the mothers who lack agency during a potentially powerful and life-changing event, and unfortunately I think that disempowerment is more common than not.

So my son, Ari Hamish, was born in March 2021 in a hospital in Brisbane, and almost nothing I had wanted to happen happened. But he was there, and I was completely and utterly in love. I kissed my son's little face, counted his toes and his fingers, then gave in to sleep. I could have slept for a hundred years if they'd let me. I was completely drained, but buzzing with the thought that I had done it – all the hard stuff was over. He was here, and everything was fine.

I wish this is how I could end this book, but alas, I cannot – because everything was not fine.

EVERYTHING IS GOING TO BE FINE ... RIGHT?

'Well, if you're happy to go home now, that's fine by us.' The midwife was annoyed with me by this stage. Actually, I reckon I had been annoying for her since I had arrived only hours earlier. This was the midwife who had been unbelievably dismissive during my agonising labour for a baby with a head so huge I had to be induced two weeks early. And when I say 'huge', I mean enormous. And when I say 'enormous', I mean unforgivable.

I think everyone was stunned he hadn't ripped me completely in half (I must have a gigantic fudga) and that he seemed totally fine, so they were happy to send me on my way. He was born at 5am, and I was home in time for a late lunch. I wanted to leave that place as quickly as possible because I felt invisible there and I needed validation that I existed. It was Covid times so visitors weren't allowed and I was desperate to get home to my girls to show them what I'd made for them. (FYI: I'd made their brother; I didn't have time to sculpt a vase.)

I also felt powerful leaving so early. It felt like a weird feminine flex, like working full-time and still nailing Book Week, or being effortlessly slim despite eating carbs at dinnertime. We can deny it until we're blue in the face, but there is *always* a competition to 'out-woman' other women, and how we birth a baby is right up there, with one of the highest scores.

I wanted to leave the hospital and for people to say, 'WOW! You went home after only a few hours? You're so brave and strong and did we mention INSPIRATIONAL?!' It feels dumb admitting it, but I'm pretty ready to admit to embarrassing things now because I'm too tired to pretend otherwise. Also, though I didn't know it at the time, a little part of me was caught up in the ridiculous celebration of women who breeze through birth 'naturally'. I had needed an epidural for Ari's birth and I was disappointed in myself, even though I had always high-fived friends who had opted for one. Considering the enormity of his head, I can't believe I wasn't given the option of a C-section, so it's wild to me that I thought I could do it without numbing the lower half of my poor old body. By the way, some of you may not know this, but the numbing can wear off for the pushing part – in which case, you get to feel all of that – so I wouldn't ever worry about a woman having a pain-free birth. If the pain isn't during, it's after, which is simply wonderful news for any woman who is yet to experience childbirth. You're welcome.

Self-righteous women who gatekeep the glory of birth with arbitrary rules that focus on female suffering piss me off to no end. I am ALL FOR women having home births, drug-free births – whatever they want – but the second someone brags about their birth as if they achieved a more 'authentic' birth, I'm out. I once shared an office with an insufferable woman who was always telling our heavily pregnant colleague how to be pregnant and what to expect in labour. She'd only had one baby, so it was crazy to me that this woman thought she understood every pregnancy and birth, but I guess every workplace has at least one sanctimonious arsehole (in teaching, there are bloody heaps of them). Anyway, my heavily pregnant co-worker waddled into work late one morning after an appointment with her midwife, and the know-it-all said loudly, 'Oh, I remember those appointments. I loved my birth, actually. I did it without any pain relief and afterwards every doctor and midwife on the ward came in to congratulate me for being the only woman that day who gave birth naturally!'

What. A. Flog.

I think she was expecting the office to give her a standing ovation, but all I wanted to yell was, 'Firstly, AS IF the midwives gave a fuck how that baby came out, and WHO CARES if you had pain relief or not!' But I didn't. Because, like every cancelled comedian and alcoholic radio host says, you can't say anything anymore. I just stared at her until I made her uncomfortable enough to return to her desk. Then I said, 'Well, I had an epidural for Olive and nothing for Edie, and both births were bloody awful. Do whatever you need to do, just get that baby out.' I had been a teacher for years by that stage, and that was maybe the greatest lesson I'd ever given.

I digress ...

Leaving the hospital after a few hours didn't feel risky because I figured a lot of women don't go to the hospital at all. Many women have home births, or shoot a baby out of their fudga in the forest or accidentally have them in the office toilets, so having a baby in a hospital and leaving a few hours after seemed super safe to me. I mean, I've done much riskier things, including eating Chinese food that had been in my mum's fridge for weeks, plucking my own eyebrows in Year 8, and having a baby with someone I'd only just met. This didn't feel risky at all.

When I returned home, my mum, parents-in-law and girls were so excited to meet Ari. I mean, why wouldn't they be? It still feels wild that I'd created a whole new person from my body and gifted him to them as their new family member. Women don't get enough praise for that. If you have a sibling and you like them, remember your mother made them for you. If you have a sibling and you don't like them, remember that's probably your dad's fault somehow. You simply cannot fight science.

Seven-year-old Olive and five-year-old Edie ran down the front stairs and excitedly peeked into the bundle of blankets holding their teeny brother. I felt like a five-year-old bringing their favourite drawing home. In fact, it wasn't too dissimilar, because they all had to gush over how perfect my creation was, even though his head was colossal.

Once we got inside, everyone was welling up. Lukasz's mum, Jola, gushed over her first grandson and kissed his forehead, and the three grandparents huddled around scanning his face to see which family he looked more like. It still chokes me up thinking about how much they love their grandchildren, and how proud I am to feel like I was a part of creating that love. It isn't a unique theory that grandparents see their grandchildren as second chances for them to remedy the perceived mistakes they made with their own children. My kids are so lucky to have generational affection because I know how important Nan's love was to me. It still is, even though she is long gone.

Finally, Jola in a thick Polish accent, 'You named him Ari?'

Here we go. I was waiting for this. When Olive was born, Lukasz texted the family to announce her name. Jola called him and said, 'You mean Olivia, right?'

'No, Mamus,' he replied, 'Olive is her name.'

'Like for pizza? *Nie*!'

Edie's announcement was even worse. I thought Edith would be right up her alley because 'Edita' is a strong Polish name, but apparently she has beef with someone in Poland called Edita, so we accidentally ruined her name by not checking who in the world Jola liked and didn't like. Rookie mistake!

So here we were at our third shot of naming a child Jola might approve of, and we missed once again.

'Yep,' I said rubbing my soft tummy. 'We like the name Ari.'

She stood there, tight-lipped, as if words of criticism were crawling up her throat and bashing on the inside of her teeth.

I took the bait. I had to. 'And do *you* like the name Ari?'

She took a moment to think and said, 'What were the other choices?'

She's doing well, I thought. She's showing more restraint than usual. 'I loved Sidney and Arthur, but Lukasz liked Abraham and Moses. The only other one we both liked was Albert.' I looked at her, waiting for her to hate all of them.

'Oh, Albert is good. You should have chosen Albert.' She looked pleased with herself, as if she'd given me a compliment when she'd usually dished out an accidental insult, a quintessential Polish boomer trait.

'But we didn't choose that one, Jola, we chose Ari.' I looked at her looking lovingly at Ari and reminded myself that, even though she might never seem satisfied with any of my decisions, she was in love with my creations, despite their revolting names. What makes this story even funnier to me is that a few years later her daughter, my genuinely perfect sister-in-law, had a son and named him Albert. We thought Jola would be over the moon about it, but it turns out she wasn't very happy with the name after all - which means she either changed her mind or *really* didn't like the name Ari. Bless her Polish socks.

Like Hels, Jola is truly a magnificent woman. They both have made it abundantly clear that they will love my children unconditionally, and really, isn't that the most important role of a grandmother? I respect them both deeply, but I hope that when I become a nan, I remember just how unique motherhood is to each woman. It can't be taught, and advice should always be given as a suggestion. I want to remember that the generation of mothers before me did it differently, and the generation of mothers after me will also do it differently, and that's okay. If I can give my children anything it would be the patience to watch them turn into the parent they need to be. I don't think it's a particularly uncommon experience for a grandmother to think she knows more about motherhood than a new mother does, and I probably will experience pangs of 'What the hell are they doing with my grandchild?' But I hope this paragraph acts as a future reminder to me that any judgement I throw towards a new parent will feel like a direct attack. I should know – I was given a lot of 'advice' about my parenting from loads of different people from the generation before me, and at the start it stung. Now, when I'm given 'advice' I just bury it deep within me and remember I'll outlive all these critics, so I just let them say whatever they want.

Anyway, I digress ...

It was so lovely to be home and it was sensational to not be pregnant anymore. I hated pregnancy with the fire of a thousand suns, so to have my body back (kind of – as if it was ever truly mine to begin with) was paradise. I was totally and completely up myself and there were moments when I could *almost* ignore the pangs of terror that had taunted me from the moment I found out I was pregnant. I closed my eyes, held my breath and waited to see if I could feel or hear my anxiety rising again. It was there, but thankfully it was still quite dull and the faint optimist in me tried to reassure myself this might be the loudest it would get. The realist in me knew that I wasn't going to emerge from this unscathed, and unfortunately that part of me was bang on.

The worst part about knowing you're going to lose your footing is not knowing how hard the fall will be. You know when you watch someone trip, their face contorts in the most outrageous way, not only from shock but from the fear of how much it's about to hurt. I could feel myself sitting on the edge of a crumbling cliff face, hoping that this time it could withstand me. Could I be so lucky?

As I stood in my sun-drenched Brisbane home with my three perfect children, I couldn't help but give a gentle nod to the possibility of The Noise returning. I shuddered and tried to shake it off, which was as effective as a midwife saying, 'You're going to have to pull yourself together!' Lest we forget.

If there was a right and wrong way to have a baby, there was certainly a right and wrong way to experience a newborn, and I was on my third shot at getting it right. Ari was soft, pink and fresh and he offered me the opportunity to show everyone who'd worried about me in the past that motherhood could be a seamless experience for me. I mean, I wasn't facing the challenge of entering motherhood this time – the girls had already solidified my role as a mother. Surely this time I had a fighting chance of getting through the newborn stage intact. Surely I wouldn't sing at the park or redevelop a CrossFit addiction or find myself drowning in self-perceived failure. Surely my lived experience would make up for something! Wouldn't it?

Day turned into night and night turned into day and lo and behold we had made it to the afternoon of day two of Ari's life and all of the wheels were still on. Maybe the biggest hurdle I would have with this baby was getting Jola used to his name? Maybe I would be okay? Maybe everything would be totally fine! And it was ... until it wasn't.

PLEASE WAKE UP

Day two of having a third baby was surreal. The wait was over. No more hospital visits or people rabbiting about his massive head. I could lie on my stomach, if I ever put Ari down (which I didn't, but I could if I really wanted). Day two already and everything seemed totally fine ...

During the night, he was sleeping for long stretches, and when I woke him to feed, he would suck for a few seconds and drift off again. I kept tickling his feet and blowing air on his face to keep him awake, and it would work briefly but then he'd zonk out again. The optimistic side of me tried to convince myself that my milk must have been really rich this time around and he was full as an egg, but the realist in me knew something was awry.

Please wake up.

We got through to morning and I told Lukasz that Ari slept too heavily. Lukasz rolled his eyes and said, 'Didn't you want a good sleeper?' I felt a hot flush of anxiety – he was right. Maybe I was just being impossible to satisfy? Maybe I was overreacting?

But I wasn't. It got to the point that he wasn't waking at all, and Mum came into my room and lifted his eyelid. His eyes rolled back in his head.

Helen, a nurse of fifty years, calmly said, 'Okay, off you pop to the hospital now. Quickly, Bron, he needs a doctor.'

There it was. The woman who never panicked about anything, the nurse who never went to the doctor herself, was suggesting the hospital. I bloody knew there was something wrong! The Noise was at full volume now and I couldn't hear anything Lukasz was saying. I told him we had to go, and I got in the back of the car and held my breath and Ari's tiny three-day-old hand. He slept deeply the whole way there and stopped flinching when I tickled his feet. My skin felt like it was on fire. I bawled my eyes out and whispered phrases that I thought might comfort him, but were really just for me. 'I'm sorry, baby boy, we will get the doctors to help you. Mummy is here and I will make sure they fix this. I'm so sorry, I don't know what I've done wrong.' The drive took forever, and every time Lukasz stopped at a red light I felt like I could have screamed. For the entire journey, I didn't take my eyes off my baby, and for the entire journey he remained perfectly still.

Please wake up.

Lukasz pulled up at the emergency department of the shittiest-looking hospital I've ever seen in my life and I asked, 'Where the fuck are we?' Not only had he adhered to the road rules for the entire trip, but he'd taken us to the wrong hospital. Hot with rage and helpless with fear, I stopped talking. There was no time to argue with him and certainly no time to drive to the lovely new Children's Hospital suburbs away, so I got out and hoped there were some doctors in there who could magically fix him. They had to. There was literally no other option.

I tried to walk in, but there was a security person at the door asking me to sign my name for Covid reasons. I had my arms full of a lifeless baby and I just said, 'No.' I walked in and had to wait in line behind a family who all wore matching Broncos Oodies and it felt like they were talking in slow motion. The admin lady at the triage counter asked me to come over and I couldn't speak. I was crying too hard to tell her what was wrong, so any word that came out had to climb over a mountain of fear and desperation. I somehow communicated to her I needed to see a doctor straight away, and she said, 'Yep, I can see that. One more question, what is his religion?'

WHAT? Who gives a shit?! I looked at her, stunned, but no words came out. A doctor must have heard what was happening and came to many rescue. She was young, blonde and sprightly and pretended to not notice how much of a mess I was.

'Well, well, well, what's going on here, huh? What's this little bubba doing?' She took him from my arms and put him on a hospital bed gently to not wake him up, which was entirely unnecessary as he wasn't showing any signs of stirring. On the adult-sized bed, he looked tinier than ever. 'Oh, he's a sleepyhead, isn't he?'

'He won't wake up!' I blurted out. 'Help him!'

She smiled at me and walked swiftly over to the wall where she hit a big red 'EMERGENCY' button and we were immediately surrounded by nurses and doctors pulling his clothes off, poking him, prodding him and speaking quickly to one another. The sprightly blonde doctor perched herself on the end of the huge bed and tried to get me to pay her some attention. They started to become more aggressive with him, and yet he remained completely silent. One doctor with bright blue runners took control. The volume in my head ramped up, which signified the start of both the loudest and, ironically, the most silent time of my life.

The blonde doctor tilted her head and offered me a weak smile. 'It's okay,' she said. 'This doesn't look like a sick baby to me. He might just need a kickstart. Sometimes that happens.'

Does it? I'd never heard of a baby needing a 'kickstart'. Was she pissing in my pocket? I found flowery doctors like her insufferable: they always had a patronising persona and spoke to me like I was a confused toddler at a Wiggles concert. I was dubious, but I held on to the sliver of hope she offered because it was really all I had to hold on to before freefalling.

'Did he bump his head?' she asked.

'No! I haven't put him down!'

'When did you notice him being this lethargic?'

'Last night. Maybe three am?' The words felt like thick lumps of mud being pulled out of my mouth. She was struggling to understand me, but generously pretended I was calm and controlled.

'Three am?' She glanced at her watch and then over at the doctor in blue shoes.

Fuck. That was more than seven hours ago. I knew there was something wrong with my newborn baby and I waited *seven long hours* before I sought help? This was entirely my fault. The noise in my head grew louder, and shame wrapped itself around me so tight that I thought I was going to die then and there. Where the fuck was Lukasz?

'Do you have a partner, or are you here alone?'

I pointed towards the car park and she whispered to a nurse to go find him. I hated that. I needed them to use their skills on my son. Lukasz was a grown man, he didn't need anything, and by this point I was livid with him. My brain revelled in this state of panic and in the horrific possibilities that lay ahead. It offered up the suggestion that the staff were getting Lukasz to come say goodbye to his son, and my knees buckled.

Please wake up.

The nurse returned with Lukasz, who frantically tried to explain that the security guard wouldn't let him in because Covid regulations meant each patient was allowed only one guardian. A flicker of rage interrupted my panic: this fucking pandemic had fucked my birth and now it was impacting the care of my tiny son and I was FINISHED WITH IT! The rage was quickly swallowed by a tidal wave of anxiety as they discovered Ari's blood-sugar levels were NIL and the doctor with the blue runners grabbed a full syringe of glucose and squirted the entire contents into his mouth. What did that mean? None of the medical team, aside from the blonde doctor and the doctor with blue runners, looked me in the eye.

The doctor with the blue runners was a robust character who kept saying dumb things to me that her colleagues pretended they didn't hear. Like, 'Oh, this is a classic boy thing to do! Boys are such drama queens! We girls get such a bad reputation for overreacting, but look at this little guy! He's being so silly!' No one laughed. I definitely didn't. I wondered if she was looking at the same 'drama queen' as I was – my three-day-old, lifeless son. What the hell was she talking about?

By this stage the faint optimistic part of my frazzled brain was long gone and all that was left was noisy electricity and fire. My brain now felt like Jafar at the end of *Aladdin*, when he turns into a gigantic, muscly red genie who towers over everyone and laughs down at them mockingly. It told me that most of the staff were avoiding eye contact with me because Ari wasn't ever going to wake up and it was all my fault. I wouldn't want to look a baby killer in the eyes either. Oh my god, have I somehow killed my baby?

PLEASE wake up!

Lukasz rubbed my back to try to calm me down enough to answer the blonde doctor's questions, but my words were now fat slugs, impossible to get out and even harder to understand. Lukasz and the blonde doctor repeated what they thought I was saying until two senior doctors came in: two identical small women with glasses and mousy brown hair. Both were slight and serious, with thin lips and a calmness about them that made me feel violent. How the fuck were they calm?! My baby wasn't waking up and they gave him glucose or some shit.

PLEASE WAKE UP!

One of the small doctors took over handling Ari and the other small doctor took over questioning me.

'How was the labour?'

'Fine,' I lied. 'Well, it was harder than I expected, but no one seemed to think it *wasn't* fine. He has a huge head.' My volume was all over the place. I was either too loud or too quiet, and they all worked as a team to decipher what I was saying.

She looked back at him and up at the other doctor. 'Macrocephaly.'

'Yes!' I blurted out. I was still ugly-crying, but words seemed to slip out a little easier by now. 'That's the one. Can you help him? Why isn't he waking up?!'

PLEASE! WAKE UP!

She ignored my questions and turned back to me. 'How was the pregnancy?'

'I had to have extra scans because of his head, but he was fine when he came out.' I was frantically trying to read the doctors' faces, but they were giving me nothing. In my head, Jafar grew bigger. I should have noticed something when he was born. Why did I not come in at 3am? Why the fuck are we at the shitty hospital and not the good one?

'Have you ever had cold sores?'

'Um, yes, but not recently I don't think.'

This changed the vibe in the room. The doctor in the blue runners yelled out for an antibiotic and a nurse ran for it.

My small doctor furrowed her brow. 'We will treat him for the virus that he may have contracted from your cold sore strain just to rule that out.' She looked back down at him and his lifeless body. 'But I need more information. Did you have any tests during pregnancy?'

'Yes,' I stammered. 'I had an MRI on my belly.' I started to buckle again and the words regressed to strained and wobbly versions of themselves. I wanted Lukasz to take over, but he was at a loss as to what I wanted him to say. The pregnancy was my job, and I spent most of it reassuring him that everything was fine, his head was only slightly bigger and I wasn't worried, so he shouldn't worry either.

'An MRI? Okay, did that reveal anything of interest?' By this stage all four doctors were looking at me with furrowed brows.

'It said he had a tiny bit more fluid on his brain than expected. But the neurologist said it might be fine!' I was desperately scanning their faces, looking for any signs that they had solved the case. It was in this moment that I remembered the neurologist also said that he might not be fine. The extra fluid might mean he would have a disability, but only time would tell. Apparently Day Three was the time he was referring to. I'd kept this information from Lukasz during the pregnancy because if I saw him worry it would make it a possibility, and that was unacceptable. I needed him to be okay, so I spent no time thinking he wouldn't be.

'And it might be fine,' she said calmly. 'But he should have reacted to that glucose, so we are going to do a lumbar puncture and that will hopefully give us the information we need.'

I didn't know what a lumbar puncture was, and I didn't ask. I just wanted them to do all of the things they needed to fix him now. Why were they wasting their time talking to me? I was awake! I was fine! I was not the victim here; I was probably the villain.

'Lukasz,' said the blonde doctor. 'You take Bron to get a cuppa. You guys don't need to be in there for the procedure. It's really painful for bub, so it can be quite distressing for the parents.'

How, I thought, could I get any more distressed than this?

'And try to relax, this is all classic boy behaviour!' The doctor with the blue runners laughed at her own joke and we stared back at her blankly. Please, for the love of God, fuck off.

I looked down at Ari, who remained still and silent, and went to kiss him, but remembered I held the cold sore strain, so it could have been my kisses that put him here. Jafar laughed loudly at the irony and my heart sank further into my stomach.

Please wake up.

Lukasz ushered me out of the emergency department and towards the cafeteria. The poor bastard had to look after me, the woman who had somehow broken his only son. He sat me down and my arms felt useless without Ari in them.

'What do you want, babe? A coffee?' he asked.

A coffee? No, I was breastfeeding, I thought. Then my mind screeched to a halt. Am I breastfeeding? Maybe I wasn't. Oh god, maybe, unbeknown to me, I'd fed my son for the last time.

'I don't know. What if he needs me to feed him?' I asked, and watched his face like a hawk, hoping he didn't show any of the same fears.

Lukasz looked down at me and said, 'Bron, I wouldn't worry about that now, it's just a coffee. He is going to be just fine. Please, have whatever you want.'

I didn't want anything. I wanted my son to wake up.

Please wake up.

I decided on a peppermint tea, which I didn't want, and drank it quickly despite the scorching liquid burning my mouth. I didn't care; in fact it felt right to me to have physical pain at this point. The bright lights hurt my swollen red eyes and the few people there glanced at me and looked away quickly, to save me the shame of being caught crying in public. This generous act was lost on me. I couldn't give a shit who saw me cry at that point, because it felt like I would never stop. The world was going to have to get used to me looking like this. The table was wobbly and had streaks on the faux marble where someone had wiped it down with a filthy cloth. Lukasz asked if I wanted a blueberry muffin that was wrapped so tightly in cling wrap that it reminded me of a woman being killed with a plastic bag. My brain was truly doing a number on me, even when it came to baked goods.

The tiled room seemed forgettable – insignificant even – but it was here in this poxy Brisbane hospital cafeteria that Lukasz and I had a conversation that revealed how incredible he was and how horrible I was.

Side note: I have been dreading writing this bit since I decided to write this book. Truly *dreading it. Not because it was the worst morning of my life, but because I am reliving a level of shame I didn't even think was possible. This chapter took a few goes to finish. I don't know if I'll ever read it back, but I hope it brings someone comfort and I hope even more that no one ever speaks to me about it. I haven't forgiven myself yet, and maybe I never will.*

Lukasz sipped his burnt coffee and smiled at me. 'It's okay, Bron. He's in safe hands. They're going to sort this. Everything is going to be fine.'

How could he think this? Ari's not waking up! First he drove slowly, then he took us to the wrong hospital, now he's gaslighting me. I was so alone and I resented him for not seeing just how horrific the whole thing was, especially seeing as his Polish roots often had him catastrophise the smallest of problems.

'How do you know?' I scanned his face and quickly evaluated my responsibility to him. The only thing I could do was share the thoughts Jafar was stoking, in the hope that he could make them go away. 'Lukasz, I don't think he is going to be fine. I think he is going to die or be really, really disabled.' My voice trailed off and I sobbed into my clammy hands.

I'd finally let myself sink into the thoughts I feared the most. Usually I protected Lukasz from the dark parts of my brain, but I needed him to meet me there – not to save me from them, but to sit with me there.

I pictured our life with a severely disabled child and chastised myself for thinking I was allowed three healthy kids. I'd pushed my luck and now I had ruined my entire family's life. We would need to build a ramp to the front door. We would never go on family holidays. I would have to become Ari's full-time carer, and how on earth would I not resent him for that? The girls' childhoods would have a thick black line down them – Before Ari/After Ari – and soon enough their lives would be so unrecognisable that they'd have next to no memories of 'Before Ari'. Before Ari. That was only nine months ago. I feel hot shame as I write this, but in that cafeteria I found myself regretting him. Two kids *was* enough. I'd ruined everything.

Lukasz sat upright and said confidently, 'If he is disabled we will deal with it.'

'But,' I whispered. 'I don't want to.'

Without missing a beat he replied, 'Then I'll deal with it. I'll look after him.'

I looked over at him, and he really meant it. There was no malice in his voice, no disappointment that his son's mother seemed to love his son conditionally. I don't know how he didn't immediately hate me then and there. Maybe I was hating myself enough for the both of us.

I winced. I felt like I'd been exposed as the worst mother in the universe and he would never look at me the same again. I wanted to find the words that had come out of my mouth and squash them like cockroaches, but it was too late.

'It's okay, Bron. We can do this. You can focus on the girls, I'll take care of him. We will get through this as a family, I promise.'

As cross as I had been at him for the red lights and the wrong hospital, everything shifted and I had never loved him more than in that moment. At the same time, I'd never hated myself as much. I knew he meant it. He was right – we could do this. Heaps of parents have kids with disabilities;

why did I think I was going to bypass it?

We finished our drinks and headed back to Emergency. The security guard tried to stop us from coming in, blurting out some scripted shit about how only one guardian was allowed, but I moved around him, and Lukasz, who had been calm for the entire nightmare so far, yelled, 'We have a sick baby!'

His outburst shocked and invigorated me, then it broke my heart. It confirmed he was aware this was as grim as I thought it was, but he knew one of us had to be the strong one.

We walked down the hallway, listening to children cry for various reasons, and held our breath hoping one of the cries belonged to Ari. None of them did. The lumbar puncture took much longer than they said it would. I walked in to find his tiny body curled into a ball as the doctor with the blue runners tried to shove a needle into his spine.

Please wake up.

I wanted one of the tiny senior doctors to be doing it, but they were more interested in me by this stage. I ran my teeth over my burnt tongue to ready myself for the blame. I was just as curious to learn what I'd done wrong, but I was fucking petrified to hear it. I knew there was no going back after that. They stood side by side, and their likeness would have been comical on any other day, but on this day it just annoyed me.

'Tell us more about your pregnancy. Did you take recreational drugs?'

'No!'

'Smoke cigarettes?'

'No!'

'Drink alcohol?'

Uh-oh. 'Well, every now and then I would have a glass of wine.'

One of the small doctors' expressions didn't change but the other one scribbled something in her notepad.

There it was. It was my fault. I fucking knew it.

I looked over at Ari and the doctor with the blue runners gave me the thumbs up. She'd finally finished the procedure and said, 'He's not such a drama queen after all! He was such a trooper during that lumbar puncture, he didn't even cry!' Her words hung in the air like the stench of hot compost. What the fuck was she thinking? I would have given both my legs to hear him cry at that point, which I guess would have been fine, considering the ramp I had already mentally built in our house.

The twin senior doctors quietly chatted between themselves while a nurse gave me a breast pump. I thanked her and it warmed my racing heart at this small gesture of hope. At least someone here thinks he might have another feed. If he ever wakes up again.

Please, my darling boy, please wake up.

DEALS WITH THE DEVIL

Ari and I were admitted to the shitty hospital on Easter Friday. It had been the longest day of my life, and it was only the start of the longest week I'll ever *just* survive. Lukasz kissed me on the forehead and I said he could tell the family whatever he wanted, but I gave him strict instructions to tell them not to call or message me. I wasn't exactly sure how I would respond if I were on the receiving end of someone's pity at this point, but I was certain it would be with anger. I was worried I would tell our families to get stuffed because after the insufferable pity would presumably come questions about how Ari ended up there, and surely this was somehow my fault.

To this day I don't know how Lukasz handled the families, our daughters and me so delicately yet stoically. It genuinely blows my tiny mind how this man, who usually overreacts to having a cold or any degree of uncertainty, made it seem like he'd been training for this exact moment his whole life. Personally, I had never handled anything so clumsily or without filter as I did that week and, while I make no apology for it, I have to acknowledge he didn't have the luxury of joining me. I still have no idea how he managed it, but I know for a fact that while I offered him a place next to me in the darkness, the invitation expired the second he refused it. I gave him no space to meet me where I was – there was only room for one of us to fall to bits in this mess, and he not only held my hand while I did it, but he fended off people with the best intentions who would have ultimately made it worse. I'd never been in that situation before, but Lukasz knew me so intimately that he knew exactly what I needed and put that before anything he needed, and I'll be eternally grateful for that.

Ari and I had our own room in the rundown hospital, which was a relief, but it didn't detract from how much I hated the hospital. There was peeling paint and tired posters on the stained walls, and it had nowhere near as many resources or staff as the big hospital. Still, as frustrated as I was about Lukasz accidentally taking us there, I couldn't be mad at him after he'd shown me how much better a parent he was.

I didn't get under the covers of my hospital bed; I just sat on the bed and looked at Ari, who was snug in a portable bassinet: sleeping, of course. The blonde doctor disappeared along the way, and so did one of the mousy brown ones. I was mostly relieved that the moronic doctor with the blue runners and big mouth wasn't there anymore, but part of me wished she were, because, while she often said curt things, at least she talked to me about Ari. The other doctors just seemed to be trying to calm me down while asking questions about me, the perpetrator. Still, I've had enough space from that day to realise the blue-runner doctor was a daft dickhead. Just before she signed out of her shift, she came over to me and said, 'I can see you want answers. We don't have any at the moment but, from the history you've provided us, I reckon it's his brain.' And then she was gone. My heart couldn't sink any further after that; it sat frozen in the pit of my stomach, where it stayed for longer than you would think. The phrase 'I reckon it's his brain' was on a loop in my head for days because it was the only thing I'd been told. His brain. Okay, now what?

The last remaining doctor came to see me before she, too, clocked off. She was the more talkative of the mousy duo. When she came in, I shuffled around on the bed so I could see her and Ari at the same time, and as I did I must have winced because she asked if I needed pain relief.

'Me?' I asked. My skin prickled with frustration. 'No, I'm fine.' I was fed up with questions about me. I was in a children's ward and the number of questions about me, a thirty-four-year-old woman, started to feel patronising. I wished everyone would stop looking at me or worrying about me because they were wasting valuable time. My son needed their attention, not me.

She could sense my irritation. 'Okay, I only ask because you experienced a traumatic birth three days ago. Did you want me to take a look at your stitches?'

I was stunned. Was it *only* three days ago? Did he only *just* arrive? The day itself had felt like it had gone for months; how on earth was I living normal life only yesterday? I moved tentatively on the bed to see if my stitches hurt. I'd forgotten about them, obviously, and while they definitely stung and the flesh around them throbbed, I told her nothing hurt and I was totally fine. The mousy doctor knew I was lying – I mean, unless I had a fudga the size of a doorway, I would have been experiencing discomfort, but she decided not to push it. She was starting to get it.

I didn't need anything except answers about why my baby wasn't waking up, and I know there was a large part of me that wanted to feel the pain. Not only to remind me of when he'd come out and cried that beautiful, tiny cry that I missed so much, but also to punish me for somehow making the cry vanish. This combination of shooting and dull pain was the least I could shoulder for him. It was the least I deserved.

Once the mousy doctor left my room, silence washed over everything, except The Noise in my head. That was as loud as ever, but now there were no other noises to challenge it. It was just me, my lifeless baby, the machines he was strapped to and The Noise. This was worse than I'd ever feared. The Noise was back with a vengeance, but this time I welcomed it. Without it, it would have been the deafening silence that destroyed me.

None of the doctors showed any signs they knew what was happening to him, but they assured me that they were working on it. They promised they were doing a litany of tests and tried to give me hope that this very well could be a hapless but innocuous little blip. I didn't sleep at all, despite a jolly nurse telling me I needed to. Oh, I need to sleep? Okay, silly me, please accept my most sincere apology. Night-night! Fucking. Fuck. Off. I lay awake and watched Ari in case he stirred. In case I missed something again. In case I was given an opportunity to redeem myself as his protector, as his mother.

Please wake up.

I sat on the bed and made deals with the devil. I figured it was the only thing I could do and the logical part of me by this stage was fading behind the brightening lights of madness. These deals felt so satisfying, like scratching an itch. I thought it was because I was offering assistance to his recovery, but I know now that they were just another way of punishing myself – methodically listing all my failures one by one. 'If you let my son wake up, I'll stop gossiping about people behind their backs. I'll exercise and eat well. If you let him wake up, I'll be a better daughter to my mother and I'll learn to forgive my father. I'll stop swearing and I'll be more present with my kids.' I think it's important to note that, even after Ari woke up, I didn't follow through with many of these promises, so there is a part of me that's waiting for the devil to come back and claim something. I hope it's my cold sore strain, or at the very least my tax bill.

Even if I did try to sleep, it would have been near impossible because every hour, the night nurse had to bustle in and test his blood-sugar levels in case they dropped again. He wasn't maintaining his blood-sugar levels himself, so he was on a drip. Still, the tests continued and they became my new obsession. To do the test, the nurse had to give his tiny heel a prick and take a couple of drops of his blood. Every single time, she would say, 'Sorry, bubba, this might hurt,' but he never flinched. Most of the time I appreciated the sentiment, but in my lower moments I felt patronised by the charade. I wanted to yell, 'He can't hear or feel you, you idiot!' But I bit my burnt tongue and held my breath until they left me alone with my son and The Noise.

I sat on my bed and cycled my attention through three different things: Ari, the clock and the door. The nurses appeared every hour on the hour, but the mousy doctor came only twice a day – when she started her shift and just before she left for the day. *Devil, if you make the doctor find the answers I need today, I will get rid of social media.*

I had so many questions, all of which seemed to be far too difficult for any of the nurses to answer and, when the last remaining doctor appeared, they were impossible for her to answer as well. Her aggressively calm demeanour was infuriating to me. She nodded while I asked, 'Do you know what is happening? When will he wake up?' And as soon as I'd finished speaking, her nodding would stop and she would quietly say, 'I can understand you want some answers, Bron, but unfortunately we're still in the dark here.'

WHAT?! By this stage we had been there for over twenty-four hours – that's an entire day and night to figure it out, and NOTHING?! I would harness my rage like it was a bucking bull, terrified that if I let it loose she would visit less or, worse, call child services and tell them I had anger management issues and was officially unfit to be anyone's mother. So I swallowed my fury like a hot lozenge and said, 'Please come and tell me when you find anything out. Literally anything.' I thought I meant that, but when she arrived with hot air dressed as news I wanted to burn the shitty hospital to the ground.

'Great news, Bron, he doesn't have the cold sore virus.' Oh cool, so what the hell is it then? Now that you've tainted every memory I had of kissing my son, you've shown up to tell me that actually – PSYCH! – it's not that, it's ... We don't know!

I know now that I was being extremely unfair on them. I know that nothing they were doing was to purposefully annoy me, and I know perfectly well that they were doing all they could to save my son, but when you're in the thick of it, every delay feels personal and everyone is a bloody idiot. I was furious, and I didn't know where to put my rage, so I swallowed as much of it as my body could handle and let it hiss out of me like a tiny hole on an enormous balloon.

The hours passed, and I would spend my days pumping milk, watching him and making endless deals with the devil. Lukasz would visit each day, sometimes twice, and would ask what I'd eaten. I'd lie and say a sandwich, but the self-flagellation only escalated as time went on. He never believed me because he knew me too well, but he knew better than to push me. The nurses stopped trying to make small talk because I gave them nothing to work with. The only time I tried I regretted it immediately. It was with the jolly nurse, who talked about how she was having trouble with her son at school. She'd found out through Lukasz I'd been a teacher, so she asked for my advice. It was a welcome distraction, because I was experienced in teenagers. I was not experienced in sick babies, so I was happy for The Noise to be momentarily dulled by human interaction. I asked what subjects he did like, and she said, 'History. God, he loves history. He's obsessed with it.'

'That's great,' I said. 'Some kids struggle to like any subject.'

'Yeah, I guess.' She looked down at my still and silent baby. 'I guess I can relate to you during this time because my son has been through a lot.'

My ears pricked up. Could she relate to this? Had she been sitting on anecdotal evidence that could ease this suffering? Could she be about to share with me a story that would give me enough hope for me to push through the next minute and the next until I found a way to live like this? It wasn't dissimilar to me in the bookshop with baby Olive screaming into my chest as I scanned the bookshelf for the book that had one story I could relate to, the book that would say how awful it can be, but how I would survive it. Was she my book in human form? She did not pick up on the weight I was placing on this moment and, as she folded blankets mindlessly, she went on to explain that her son loved history, which meant he went to school and could read. Oh my god, there was hope for us! I shifted my weight so I was facing her properly. She noticed me staring at her, urging her to continue.

'Yeah, he's been diagnosed with autism, which has been hard.'

Autism? I bit my burnt tongue to prevent myself from yelling, 'WHO CARES?!' I would have killed for an autism diagnosis at that point. I had taught autistic kids for years, and after I quit teaching, I tutored almost exclusively autistic kids and it was one of the most rewarding times of my life. Autism?! Yoohoo, devil! If this turns out to only be an autism diagnosis, I will never watch telly ever again. I was glaring at her, but she still thought we were bonding, so she let the drivel flow out of her like a boil being lanced. Maybe no one in her family was any good at social cues? How dare she say this to me! How dare she suggest we had anything in common. I watched her thin lips move, dug my fingernails into my palms and shut down completely. I let her ramble on about how she doesn't really care for World War II history, so it's tricky to relate to her *perfectly awake* child. Fearful of what I was capable of saying, I removed myself from the situation the only way I knew how – I closed my eyes and welcomed The Noise, drowning her out until she thought I was sleeping. Fuck. Right. Off. Please.

Some days Lukasz would come in and send me home to see the girls so I could reconnect with them and assure them everything was okay. It's hard to lie to two excitable big sisters about the baby brother they waited nine long months for, but it would have been harder to be honest with them. I ached with guilt about ruining the baby they were so excited to have and continued to elaborately picture how hard the road ahead would probably be if we were lucky enough for him to wake up again. On one of these outings away from the shitty hospital, I couldn't stop ugly-crying for the whole drive home and the tears showed no signs of slowing down, even when I pulled into the driveway. In a desperate attempt to conceal my misery, I took my daughters to the local netball courts for them to ride their bikes around so I could bawl freely behind my sunglasses. I cried harder when I saw a couple with three kids, the smallest a boy toddling around chasing his big sisters as they squealed with delight. It was a cruel coincidence to witness such unbridled joy from the exact representation of the family I thought I would have, only a few days earlier. I wanted to tell the parents they were unbelievably blessed and how awful it might have been if one of their kids went to sleep and didn't wake up, but even if I hadn't been worried about looking mental, I was crying too much to speak. Devil, if you let me give my girls a brother like that, I will go to every single one of my kids' school assemblies.

I took the girls back home and Mum was in a flurry of cleaning up board games. Her perfected avoidance and strength in a crisis meant she'd magically kept the girls oblivious to what was going on. I don't know if it's because she's known me since the day I was born (I'm pretty sure she was there), or that she just acted how she would have wanted people to act if something hard was happening to her, but she was perfect during this stage. She asked me a couple of questions about Ari, but reserved the hard ones for Lukasz. She never grabbed me by the shoulders and asked, 'Now how are *you*? How are you *really*?' That would have been very poorly received, let me tell you that for free. Hels would potter around and keep the girls happy and distracted. She would never acknowledge my puffy red eyes, or my quivering chin. The closest she got to addressing the situation with me was patting me on the hand without making eye contact and firmly saying, 'He's in the right place, my girl. Now, want a cuppa?' She would say loudly to the girls, 'We don't need Mum here, do we? We're having a great time here!' And the girls would cheer and my heart would swell with gratitude. It wasn't until well after the nightmare came to an end that she admitted she 'cried every night for that darling little boy'.

Even as I type this, I know I've never communicated to Hels how integral she was during that time. If she'd misstepped even slightly and shown me anything but perfect stoicism and gorgeous avoidance, it would have been the end of me. The times she'd let me down when I was younger paled when she was exactly who I needed her to be when I pretended I needed no one. Thank you, Mum, I am eternally grateful for you.

On the drive back to the hospital, the tears finally slowed down and I let my brain do something even more masochistic than thinking the worst – I started imagining Ari being totally fine when I got back to the room. I pictured walking in and seeing Lukasz's beaming face and noticing Ari's little arms and legs flailing about like newborn limbs do. I pictured the mousy doctor smiling, something I never saw her do, and saying, 'He's completely fine! You can all go home!' The thoughts calmed me and as I walked to his room I noticed The Noise had quietened down under the haze of hope. Devil, if he is awake when I walk in there, I will play hide-and-seek with the kids more.

I opened Ari's door and, lo and behold, I was not faced with this dream outcome. Lukasz and a new doctor I had never seen before were standing over Ari's bassinet, watching him with furrowed brows. This doctor was petite with flawless brown skin and shiny black hair. Her clothes were nicer than all of the other doctors' clothes and her shoes were stylish but sensible. She looked out of place in such a shitty hospital. By this point I looked almost too awful to be there. Was there a shittier hospital I belonged in? Lukasz looked up at me and took a deep breath. The elegant doctor tucked her long black hair behind her ears and averted her eyes.

What the fuck was happening? The news was not good. The stakes between me and the devil had risen.

THE ZOMBIE IN BED 4

'Sit down, Bron,' Lukasz said, as he walked towards me. I was frozen in the doorway, holding my breath. I knew I shouldn't have left him.

'What is going on?' I asked. All hope frayed and slipped into the darkness and The Noise ramped up so loudly that I almost needed to hold my ears.

'Hi, I'm Erica,' the elegant doctor said with a gentle smile. I didn't care who she was; I was so sick of people ignoring my questions. Whether I was actually mad then or not, the *constant* dismissal of my questions propelled me further into the abyss. 'I'm a doctor here, and I've just come in to check on this little man.'

Ari. His name is *Ari*. Not Albert, not Bubba and definitely not Little Man.

I stormed past Lukasz and the elegant doctor and looked into the bassinet at my sleeping son with tubes coming out of him. He looked exactly the same as when I'd left him, but the air in the room was ripe with dread. I looked back at the elegant doctor and frantically searched her face for any signs of what she knew and I didn't. I scraped my teeth hard along my burnt tongue, bracing myself for something worse than the worst situation I had ever found myself in – tensing all my muscles for the fall to the next level of hell. My body was pulsing with electricity and the silence left room for The Noise to grow even louder.

She said nothing, almost as if she was frightened her words would mix with my unhinged fear and electrocute us all, so she looked to Lukasz for guidance. He got that look a lot from the medical staff. He was my translator, a role he never asked for, but one he undertook without complaint. The unspoken agreement was: the nurses and doctors spoke to him, he spoke to me and I spoke to the devil.

Lukasz cleared his throat for words he didn't want to say, biding his time in an attempt to soften them. 'Well, when we were changing his nappy just now, he made some weird jolty movements, so we *think*, and we don't *know*, but maybe he was, um ...' He trailed off.

'We suspect that the jolty movements,' Erica piped up, 'could potentially have been a seizure.'

They both stared at me, waiting for a reaction.

A seizure? I was relieved. Something was happening. It might not have been good, but it was something. We had movement at the station! We had another clue for these doctors to work with!

'Oh, okay. How do we know for sure?' I asked. 'What happens now?'

They both exhaled. I didn't blame them for being terrified of me. I wasn't handling anything particularly well; in fact, I might have been the worst person that shitty hospital had ever had to deal with (brag).

'Well,' said Erica. 'Ari needs an ECG and an MRI so, because this hospital doesn't have the correct facilities, we need to transfer him to the Royal Children's Hospital.'

FINALLY! YES! I had been subtly asking for a transfer since we'd arrived and, as the hours passed, I was unashamedly announcing to anyone and everyone that we had come to the wrong hospital and we needed to be transferred immediately. They would pretend they weren't offended, but surely it must have been a bit of a sore point. Why work at the shitty hospital when there was a good one twenty minutes away? I couldn't worry about their feelings when I couldn't contain my own. It wasn't my fault they worked at the shitty one, but it was Lukasz's fault we were there. But I'd let that go, hadn't I? I had. Almost. Don't get me wrong, I'm positively certain they were all excellent doctors and nurses in their own right (albeit some with no tact or filter), but you wouldn't take your car to the best mechanic in the world if they had no tools.

Erica was invigorated by my positive reception of this information, and she rode the wave of euphoria that comes with being the bearer of good news, even if it was very murky news to the untrained ear. She smiled at Lukasz as if they'd cracked a code together and announced, 'The paramedics will come any minute to collect you and Ari, so all you have to do is pack up your things!' Before she'd finished the sentence, I was scooping my clothes into bags and scanning the floor for any rogue socks. 'Ah, no need to rush, we don't know exactly when they'll be here. They have to attend to emergencies before transfers that aren't of an urgent nature ...' She trailed off when she locked eyes with me.

'This isn't urgent?' I asked. 'Didn't you say he just had a seizure?' I had a jumper in one hand and a bag in the other.

'I said it might have been a seizure. We don't know.' She'd fucked it. She knew she had.

'So when could these paramedics come?' I asked.

'Well, let's see ...' She looked at her watch. 'It's five pm now, so I imagine they'll be here before midnight.'

'Fine,' I said, thinking she was giving me the worst possible scenario. Seven hours of waiting. I'd been in this shitty hospital for about thirty hours by this stage, so I could do another seven. Lukasz kissed me on the forehead and said he had to get going because it was Easter Sunday the next day and we hadn't been organised to buy any Easter eggs before the supermarkets sold out of them. He had to search for Easter eggs in all the service stations around Brisbane that year.

Once they had both left the room, I swiftly stuffed all of my belongings in my bag, made my bed and sat at the end of it, watching the door. Erica did say 'any minute', and my petty/hopeful brain held on to that for dear life.

Each hour a nurse would come in to check Ari's blood sugar. Stab, drip, rub. They would ask me to take my shoes off and get under the covers and assured me that they would wake me when the paramedics arrived. I ignored their suggestions and firmly declared that I was perfectly comfortable as I was.

Midnight came and still no paramedics. Fuck you, Erica. Then 1 am, 2 am, 3 am, 4 am, 5 am – no one. Finally at 6 am a paramedic knocked on my door and seemed startled to see me sitting upright, wired as a maniac. 'Oh hi, you're up early! You ready for us to take you and this little fella across town?'

The other paramedic, who was laughing with the nurses, walked in. 'Righto! Here we are! Oh, I have been looking forward to meeting this little legend all night.' They were both extroverted blonde women in their twenties and they exuded the kind of confidence oreserved for pretty women from the country. Their messy buns, blue eyes and blindingly white teeth outshone their daggy shoes and oversized belts. I was so excited to see them, even though I remained completely silent.

They popped Ari into a bassinet designed to transport babies in an ambulance. They were smitten with him and kept saying, 'He's so adorable! Oh my god, I haven't seen one this small in ages!' I knew they were trying to give me a compliment, but all I could hear was 'Babies this small don't usually get sick.' They paid my silence and helplessness no mind and tried to shake me out of it with boomingly loud and patronising statements delivered with aggressive happiness. 'My sister has a baby girl. She's so cute, but not as cute as your boy.' I knew they were trying to help, but I just wanted them to stop talking. I didn't reply to anything they said and, when we stopped at the lights, I looked at the cars next to us and wondered how many times I had unknowingly pulled up next to an ambulance with a lifeless baby and broken mother inside.

'Yeah, this job rules!' One of the paramedics announced. 'Not only is it our last job for the shift, but it's definitely the cutest! We had to deal with drunken idiots and wack-job junkies in the Valley all night.' I pictured them in the Valley late at night, wondered if their youthful beauty would have got in the way of treating gross, drunken men. It would have. Poor things. Then it struck me … Were they the 'emergencies' that got priority over my sick newborn? We waited thirteen hours after a potential seizure because some blokes drank more Bundy and Cokes than their livers could handle? I was too tired to be mad. I was numb, and I needed these women to stop talking at me.

We pulled into the lovely shiny hospital and I was ushered to a room by the paramedics and a nurse who seemed familiar with them. They had in-jokes and they fawned over Ari as if he could hear them. I ignored all of it because I didn't have the strength to listen to them anymore. Other nurses smiled at Ari as we walked past and then up at me. I felt embarrassed to be there and wondered if they knew it was my fault somehow. The room was huge and it had two other patients with their parents in there, which I immediately hated. I didn't want to share my misery so publicly. For a moment I missed the shitty hospital.

On the hospital bed was a chocolate Easter bunny and a 'My First Easter' picture book. Oh, fuck. It's Easter. I wondered if it was too early to call the girls and also what my voice would sound like now that I was officially numb. The nurse patted the bed and said, 'Well, a doctor will be here when rounds start. I'm just down the hall and the button is right here if you need me. Happy Easter!'

I looked blankly back at her. Was she joking? She averted her eyes quickly, silently acknowledging she'd said a dumb thing, and scurried off down the hall. I imagined she went to warn the other nurses about the zombie in Bed 4 with the silent baby.

The doctor arrived, introduced herself and asked me to explain what happened all over again. I didn't mind – it felt good to have a redo at the new hospital. Maybe I left something out when I arrived at the shitty hospital and this doctor would spot the problem instantly. She did his blood-sugar-level test, which read at a dangerously low level, and promptly squirted glucose into his mouth. Back to square one, but I was too numb to cry again.

Lukasz and the girls FaceTimed and I applied a thick layer of cheer to my voice. 'Happy Easter, girls! Did the Easter bunny come? Did she know we live in Brisbane now?'

'Yeah,' they said disappointedly. 'She came, but she didn't do a good job of hiding the eggs.'

'Oh?' I was usually the egg hider. I should have told Lukasz how to do it. This was my fault. The girls became distracted by their collection of eggs and ran out of frame only to be replaced by Lukasz, who looked utterly exhausted.

'How's the new hospital?' he asked with a weak and hopeful smile. I don't think I've ever seen him so drained.

'Fine. What happened to the eggs?' I whispered so as not to disturb our roommates. I wondered if I'd successfully disguised my annoyance about not being there to hide the eggs properly. The girls deserved a lovely Easter, especially this year.

'The bloody bush turkeys got to them before the girls woke up.' Classic Brisbane. We chuckled together, maybe for the first time since Ari had gone to sleep. It felt good, but I suddenly stopped myself because I knew I shouldn't be laughing in a hospital, especially in a shared room. I glanced over at the woman whose baby had a bandage on her head and the man whose baby had tubes coming out of him. Their babies were both only four months old, but they looked enormous compared to my six-day-old. Eventually I learnt that they had both been in there since birth, for different reasons, and to this day I still don't know how a human can handle four months of that hell when I barely survived a week of it. I hope they're okay now.

I could breathe a little easier at the flash new hospital because not only did it look like its equipment worked, but more doctors were coming to see Ari. He was like their new little riddle and it became a race to see who could solve him. I was more than happy to be a spectator of this competition! Finally it felt like we were getting somewhere!

Over the next few days, Ari was taken away for various testing during which he remained perfectly still and silent. He was taken in by the infectious disease team, which determined pretty quickly that he had no infections and palmed him off to the neurologists. The neurologists stuck colourful wires all over his glorious head and left them for hours to see if any seizures rolled in, but they didn't. They did an MRI, which showed two small brain bleeds that were almost certainly a result of a traumatic birth, and I resented the obstetrician and midwives who'd encouraged a natural birth. My nervous system thrived on the hunt for someone to blame, but it always circled back to me. I should have insisted on a C-section.

'These two bleeds might be nothing,' the neurologist said optimistically. 'As far as we know, most babies have brain bleeds when they're born, but we don't do MRIs on most babies.'

'So why is he asleep?' I asked.

'We aren't sure.' He walked over to Ari's bassinet and looked in. 'He might just be recovering from the brain bleeds. Sometimes we need to shut down to recover.'

'For how long?' My voice cracked.

'I can't say. Maybe a week? Maybe a month? We just have to keep him here until he does wake up.'

Until he does wake up. This was music to my ears. He seemed certain he would. I could work with this.

'And when he does? Will he be okay?'

The neurologist sat on the end of my bed. I hated when medical staff did that; it was never to say something hopeful. 'We don't know yet. We don't know how long his blood-sugar level was undetectable, and if it was undetectable for a long time, it can cause brain damage. We also don't know if these brain bleeds are harmless. I'm so sorry I can't give you a clearer answer, but we just have to wait.'

We just have to wait? You mean, *I* just have to wait. I could do that. It was my full-time job now: the zombie in Bed 4 who waits. I could do that.

He had a feeding tube, but throughout the whole time, I would try to breastfeed or bottle-feed him every few hours as if he were a healthy newborn. Some feeds lasted a few seconds, while other feeds didn't even start. The minutes turned into hours and the hours turned into days and I started to notice him drink from the bottle or my breast for longer than a few seconds. Progress! I couldn't believe it. It took all my might not to tell my roommates about it, but when I saw their sick babies, I stayed silent in my victory.

On day five he opened his eyes slowly. Only for a second or two, but he was showing signs of life I worried I'd never see again, and I was beside myself. On day six, he opened them for a few seconds longer and fed for longer. They took his feeding tube out to see if he could maintain his blood-sugar level by himself, and *he could!* I felt like we were emerging from the thick darkness into an ambient orange glow, where the world had been functioning without us.

I was careful not to get too excited. We didn't know how much damage had been done, and no doctor could say for sure what had happened or if it would happen again. One doctor referred to it as an 'episode' and I searched my memories to work out how many shows I'd watched that had only one solitary episode. Could I survive this again?

On day seven, he was awake enough for them to discharge us. Lukasz and I walked like giants down the hallway towards the elevator, past sick babies, drained parents and medical staff who wished us well. I know I've ragged on the doctors and nurses during my time there, but they are truly selfless people. It boggles my mind to contemplate how much trauma and misery they witness day in, day out, all the while having to deal with people like me, the zombie in Bed 4, who is infuriated by even the tone of their voice, the colour of their shoes or the way they breathed. Those people saved my son and I never thanked them enough for that. How could I? I didn't have any control over my emotions or reactions during that hospital stay so, at the very least, I hope I gave them a juicy bitching session in the tearoom.

We were out. We had finished the hardest week we had ever had to endure and I had lost count of the deals I'd made with the devil. I'd forgotten what most of them were, but I knew the gist of them: if the devil woke Ari up, I promised to be a better mother. And I really tried. How hard would it be to become a woman who exuded gratitude when faced with the worst-case scenario and finished with the best? Surely I would be the best mother in the world after this! I could already hear The Noise subsiding, so my feet would surely stay firmly on the ground.

And The Noise did dwindle, until it vanished completely. However, it was replaced with a noise I hated even more, something far more deafening: silence.

DESERVED DARKNESS

After the most nightmarish start to my son's life, I was home again. I found myself lying in bed with him in the exact same place as when he wouldn't wake up. A whole week of lifelessness that would go on to change me forever. Ari, on the other hand, wouldn't remember a thing.

The hospital stay was only a week, but it remains the longest week of my life. A week when my son would not wake up, when the nurses pitied me, and the doctors scratched their heads as to what was wrong with this tiny baby. When he did wake up, they saw no need to keep us there, so we were discharged and went home thinking, 'Okay, what the actual fuck just happened?'

I didn't reply to messages or answer my phone in the hospital because I knew people wanted answers I couldn't give them and, even if I could, I couldn't speak longer than a sentence before crumbling into a blubbering mess. I made a firm separation of 'us and them' when I was in hospital. 'Us' consisted of Lukasz, Ari, me and the other devastated parents in the room. I include them because I never received their pity, which I was so happy about. Misery is better when it's shared with someone who knows it intimately – even if they are a complete stranger.

'Them' was literally everyone else.

But the nightmare was over and I was now lying in bed with Ari as he slept, now less soundly. I watched him and wondered if that whole week was just a dream. They were hinting at him not waking up, at me having accidentally broken him in utero or birth. How was he tucked alongside me, squirming and readying for a feed? How was I so lucky that I got out of that hospital with a baby who might be totally fine? Did one of the deals I made with the devil work? If so, which one?

You'd think once they discharged you, with a shrug and a pat on the back, you would be over the moon. A story you can laugh about at the dinner table the following week and bring up during long drives. 'God, that was a bloody awful week, and how lucky are we, huh?! Oh my god, remember the hospital food? Yuck!'

But we didn't. It's a bit of a blur now, but I do remember not buying this lucky break. I was due hardship after announcing to the gods that two healthy children wasn't enough for this greedy pig. I was the Veruca Salt of motherhood. 'I want another one now! I want another healthy, perfect baby who will meet all their milestones at the right time and will love me unconditionally! NOW!' This level of greed was surely met with some kind of wrath. I've never been religious, but after an entire week at the hospital with only a silent limp baby and my own thoughts, I came up with some wild stuff. My brain was given free rein to punish me in there, and it didn't hold back.

For weeks after we got home, I waited for Ari to go to sleep and have another 'episode', a term that made Ari sound like a dramatic 1950s housewife who would drive her car into the river if someone criticised her dinner. An episode? The term implied that there would be more and that was absolutely terrifying. I had been pushed into a corner of broken glass without shoes and told to say thank you.

I rarely slept. Instead I spent the nights watching him sleep. If I slept longer than a couple of hours at a time, guilt would wash over me and I'd think, 'I mustn't be that worried about him if I can sleep. What kind of mother can sleep through this kind of dread?' And if he woke me up in the night, I would feel a pang of dread, just like anyone has when awoken from their sleep, but this was quickly replaced with guilt for choosing sleep over him. I constantly reminded myself that when I was in the hospital I would have given anything to hear that cry again. And then I would pick him up and feed him with both gratitude and shame.

These punishments would come thick and fast because I knew deep down that his illness, whatever it was, was definitely my fault somehow. How could it not be my fault? I wanted him, I grew him, I birthed him, I fed him and, somewhere along those lines, I must have hurt him.

Lukasz never accused me of this. In fact, he was a saint during the hospital stint and, for someone who often lives his life with his foot endearingly wedged in his mouth, he said everything right during that nightmare. I would have remembered if he'd said the wrong thing because it felt like I was rolled in honey and any raised eyebrow, mild insinuation or ambiguous question stuck to me so I could ruminate over it instead of sleeping. He kept me upright, he dealt with the families, he passed on messages to social workers who were worried about me. (Well, kind of – I told him to tell them to 'fuck right off', but he just told them 'Thank you, but, respectfully, there is no way she will want to speak to you'.) He was so calm when I was the exact opposite, and once we got home and he could see I was eating enough to survive, he let himself slip. He needed to. He needed to let himself process what we'd just experienced. I found him crying by himself a few times, tucked away somewhere secret. It was different to how I did it – I cried unreservedly the whole way to the hospital and didn't stop until I ran out of tears. That takes ages, I found out.

Once I noticed the chink in Lukasz's optimistic armour, I saw it as my cue to put on my own. I owed him some positivity after a week of telling him the world was over. So I tried. And I tried. And I tried. But I was stripped of cheer and, instead of laughing my way around the house, I went into myself. I made a little cocoon for my tiny baby and me, and I offered scraps of myself to my two beautiful daughters, and even less to Lukasz. The girls gobbled up whatever I offered and, I assume, chalked my change in mood up to just being knackered. I'm glad they had each other during that time, otherwise it would have been pretty lonely.

Weeks passed and the 'episode' seemed less likely to happen again. Ari was eating and sleeping like any other newborn, which felt like all of my prayers had been answered. But I felt overwhelmed with unworthiness at this turn of events. That week had chipped away at my very core and forced me to evaluate all the things I'd done wrong in my life, leaving me to surmise that this tragic turn of events was my chickens coming home to roost. Now that he was fine, I wondered if the universe had got it all wrong. Why did I get three healthy babies when much better people got none?

I felt myself slipping deeper and deeper into darkness and feeling absolutely powerless to fight it. I'd spent my final pregnancy fearing the flames of postnatal anxiety only to be met with the damp darkness of postnatal depression but, again, I had no idea. The entire nine months I'd lived in fear that I would turn into the worst version of myself again and, as far as I could tell, that version of myself wasn't here. Still, it was a different version. Surely this was temporary, though? I was just recovering from the biggest scare of my life; it was normal to have a bit of backlash, right?

I spent my days on the couch feeding Ari and using my body as his mattress. I figured if I could feel him breathing then obviously I was helping him breathe, so I never put him down, not even during the night. I made a deal with Lukasz that I would have Ari until 4am, and then he would wake up and take him so I could have some sleep. That sleep lasted until 5.45 am, when Lukasz went to the gym, (CrossFit, if you can even believe it?) which was his attempt at keeping his mental health intact. Even though resentment pumped through me, I couldn't chastise him for it. He had held our life together for that week, and also had never blamed me for whatever I did to hurt our son.

The days were long, but the nights were much longer and I would dread the sun going down. Even on my third baby, I still didn't know how to get through a night without an onslaught of feelings, from helplessness to frustration. Then, when the sun came up, I would catch a glimpse of myself in the kitchen window and would want to bawl my eyes out. Again, I didn't recognise that woman. Who had I become?

I went to Lukasz's sister Kasia's baby shower with the girls and left Ari at home with Lukasz because I couldn't stomach twenty long minutes of him crying in his car seat. I didn't know if he was going to cry, but I knew my nervous system couldn't handle even the risk of it. At the party, women floated around with champagne glasses filled with either orange juice, champagne or both: a mimosa for those brunch babes out there. My throat tightened when I walked in: I couldn't match the cheery vibes of the day no matter how hard I tried.

I snatched a mimosa from the kitchen bench before anyone could offer an orange juice and drank it ferociously, in the hope that it would inject some life into me. It didn't. My well-meaning mother-in-law asked if I had just drunk alcohol and I didn't have the energy to lie. I was not only the driver of her two small granddaughters, but also the breastfeeding mother of her tiny grandson. The buzz of the mimosa didn't kick in, but shame certainly did.

The baby shower was filled with colourful decorations and wholesome games of guessing the unborn baby's name and weight. I stared down at my paper and failed to think of a single name for a boy or a girl. Olive and Edie guessed names and asked me to write them down, but I couldn't focus on what they were saying, so I just wrote 'Matilda' and immediately felt stupid for guessing a name they might not choose. I apologised to Kasia for not bringing her brother, and wished I had been the one to stay home with the baby, though my arms and chest felt so relieved to be empty. As lovely as Kasia is, I knew I wasn't the one she wanted there. Lukasz is her Hamish, so why did I show up? Plus I looked like Charlize Theron in *Monster*, so I was almost definitely bringing down the aesthetic. I felt sheepish being there, even though everyone went above and beyond to make me feel welcome, which didn't make sense to me because I didn't even want to be near me.

I spoke to a woman about my hospital visit and tried to be blasé about it, but everything I said hit like a hammer. 'He just went to sleep and didn't wake up. For a whole week. I thought he was going to die or that when he woke he would be severely disabled, but we think he's alright now. I mean, he could still be really disabled – they haven't ruled that out – but at least he's not dead. How have you been anyway?' Cool vibes, Bron!

The longer I stayed, the more certain I was that I should not have left the house. I needed to be in my home and I needed to stay there forever. My failure to be anything but a wet blanket at my abundantly kind and warm sister-in-law's baby shower was the validation the darkness in me was looking for.

I didn't stay long. The relief of not holding Ari was overridden by the guilt of wanting a break from him. Hadn't I pleaded with the gods to bring him back to life? What the hell was wrong with me? After some painful conversations with people I kind of knew who pretended I looked good after having a baby so recently, I pulled the pin. I said my goodbyes, piled my girls into the car and drove the twenty short minutes home. I hated every red light for keeping me from my son and every green light for getting me back to him.

Full disclosure: I am writing this book not in the order I will publish it in, but in the order I can stomach on the day. This chapter has been the hardest one to write so far, and I haven't even written the hospital one yet, or the one where I met the woman at the park. I'm only writing this one now because my editor said I need to hurry the hell up if I want to meet my deadline. So here it is. Writing it feels almost as awful as living it. But it must be written because I owe that to my past self – the woman who thought she would never come back to life. This part is for her.

I got home and scooped Ari back into my arms. It was tense between Lukasz and me because we were both exhausted and struggling to recover from the hospital nightmare. So we became strangers under the same roof with three healthy babies we desperately wanted. He became an exercise fanatic, with a trauma he couldn't talk about because he lived with a woman he didn't recognise (hard relate), and I became a version of myself that was much worse than I could have ever imagined.

Those days were dark, and for a while each day they grew darker. I know now I was spiralling into a madness completely unfamiliar to me.

STOP ASKING IF I'M OKAY

Mother's Day was approaching and the girls were busily making art for me at their school. It would be my first Mother's Day as a mother of three, and I was dreading it. In the past it had been my favourite day of the year, but now it felt patronising. Why was it suddenly such a charade?

Mum went back to her life in Canberra with her usual 'Righto! See you next time!' Hels never showed me a flicker of doubt or concern when Ari was in hospital, but when I got home with him, she kissed his forehead and said, 'Oh, thank god. I thought we were going to lose this one.' This moment popped into my head every so often, along with the bleakest moments of Ari's 'episode'.

In the first week home, I was riding the high of relief. I found myself constantly ranting at Lukasz about how lucky we were. 'Look at him! He's awake and feeding! I can't believe it!' Over and over again. He would appease me because not only was he grateful, but he was watching a roller-coaster slowly ascend and was waiting for it to come down again.

I had read somewhere that you should talk about your fears if you want to avoid postnatal anxiety, so I spoke freely about how awful the experience was, even to the mums at the school gates whom I had only just met. This exposure therapy of sorts had mixed results. The Noise had still not returned, but I was picking the infected scab of a wound I didn't know how to treat. Days turned into weeks, and my relationship with Lukasz became more fractured as we tended to our own versions of PTSD. Without his immediate care, I didn't know how to look after myself, which for a stubborn mule like me was a bitter pill to swallow.

I was struggling and had absolutely no reason to be. I was home and my baby was completely fine. I felt ashamed that I couldn't embrace life to the fullest, as if I'd been given a piece of chocolate cake in front of a starving man and turned my nose up at it. Nothing made sense.

Mum came back to visit a month after she had left and noticed straight away that I was flat as a tack. I didn't have the energy to dye my hair, let alone brush it, and the muscles in my face felt paralysed. I watched telly all day and never laughed at the comedies or cried at the tearjerkers. I felt completely numb, until I had to leave the house and then my skin felt like it was burning. So I didn't leave the house, not unless Ari had an appointment with the GP. Mum suggested I talk to the GP about my low mood, but I scoffed at her. I didn't need a doctor – I was totally fine. I might have looked like Ozzy Osbourne after a big night (RIP), but couldn't she see how lucky I felt?

On one of the visits to my new Brisbane GP, she asked if I was okay.

'Me? I'm fine.' Not this shit again. It was during Covid, so we both had to wear face masks but I could tell she was giving me a tight smile, and she could probably tell I was gritting my teeth. I avoided eye contact and focused all my attention on my newborn baby, hoping she would do the same. I willed her to stop looking at me, to stop analysing me, to stop feeling *concerned* about me. Pity has always been my nemesis, but pity I didn't think I deserved felt even worse. *Please* stop looking at me, lady. Finally she took the hint, or I had convinced her I was okay (unlikely), and she went back to assessing Ari.

As she was writing up her notes, I sat there impatiently. 'So,' she said. 'I was hoping you would quickly do this survey for me. It's no big deal, every mother with a new baby has to do it.' Her eyes were glued to her computer screen and she was reeling this information off as if it was the most boring part of her job.

I rolled my eyes. 'How long will it take? I need to get him home.' We both looked down at Ari, who was lying calmly in my arms.

'Not long at all! We'll zoom through it. You hold him, I'll read the questions, and you answer as honestly as you can. There are no wrong answers! Does that sound okay?'

It sounded like a trap. I suddenly felt suspicious of her intentions, and wondered if the hospital, either the shitty one or the flash one, had put her up to this.

'Do I have to?' I asked.

'It only takes a minute. Here, I've got it right in front of me and it's only ten very straightforward questions. Ready?'

I was not ready. But I was here, and Ari wasn't crying. Plus, I figured I would look guilty of something if I refused to do it. Like when a criminal demands to see a warrant before letting the police look in their shed. Guilty as sin!

'Um, I suppose. Okay, please be quick, he's getting restless.' The GP and I both ignored the fact that he definitely wasn't.

'In the past seven days, I've been able to laugh and see the funny side of things: as much as I always could, not quite as much now, definitely not as much now, not at all?' She kept her eyes steadily on the computer screen.

Gosh, how long had it been since I'd laughed? I'd returned to work as an amateur comedian and had managed to make people laugh, but I couldn't work out why. Nothing was funny at the moment. I figured they were laughing because they felt sorry for me. 'Not at all,' I said, numb.

'Okay!' she said cheerfully. 'Next question! I've looked forward to enjoyment of things: as much as I ever did, rather less than I used to, definitely less than I used to, not at all?' Again, she stared at her computer.

Looked forward to things? What was there to look forward to? I guess I couldn't wait for Ari to not be a baby anymore. I looked forward to him being at least four years old. Does that count? I decided it did. 'As much as I ever did,' I said firmly.

Her eyebrows raised. She didn't believe me, but she certainly didn't challenge me on it. The test went on and on, and I offered both truthful and confused answers to questions I only half-listened to. My skin tingled and burned from being so far from my home, so I was just saying anything to be allowed to leave.

The GP twisted her wedding ring as she looked at the results and probably wondered how to break it to me that I did not score very well. 'Okay, now the results are showing me that you are quite depressed, Bron. Does that sound accurate to you?' She was speaking so calmly and gently, that I could barely hear her. The Noise nudged its way into the room and Ari started to writhe. Could he hear it too?

'Nope, I'm actually fine. I have to go.' I stood up and my handbag tipped over and the contents spilled onto the floor. I was tempted to just leave it there.

'Okay, I believe you,' she lied. 'Unfortunately I have to see Ari again tomorrow because it's important for us to be measuring his head quite consistently.'

'Again?' I said. 'Tomorrow?'

She nodded. 'Yep, it'll be quick, I promise.'

I went to the reception to pay and found myself being ignored by three awful women who acted like they couldn't hear or see me. They were chatting among themselves about what they hoped to get for Mother's Day and how it had better not be the same boring stuff as usual. I stood there glaring at them. I already felt so useless, and these dragons were making me feel invisible too. I wanted to yell at them but I felt like I was under investigation by the GP, so I dug my nails into my palm and waited impatiently. Eventually one of the women looked up at me and said, 'Oh, the doctor bulk-billed that for you.' Finally, a win.

I went home and immediately felt better, being in my lounge room. I ranted at Mum about how ridiculous the test was and how incompetent the GP was. I was livid I had to go back the very next day, but as if I wasn't going to. I wouldn't risk Ari's health ever again.

The next visit seemed like a pantomime. She measured his head and gently asked me how I was. 'Stop asking if I'm okay,' I said bluntly.

'Sorry, I just remember you mentioned you had postnatal anxiety with your first two babies, so it's common for it to return with consecutive babies.'

'I don't have anxiety. I can't hear The Noise most of the time. Everything is eerily quiet.' I felt like that should have been enough.

'The Noise?' she asked.

Christ almighty. 'Yeah, it was really noisy when I had anxiety. It's silent now. I'm fine. I'm completely fine.'

She looked at me, unconvinced. 'Remind me, what was your experience with antidepressants again?'

I was getting annoyed now. I did not want medicine. All memories of antidepressants ever being helpful had somehow vanished and I was left with only the memories of the three weeks of withdrawals I experienced when I stopped them. Logic had faded and all that was left was a deep darkness I was strangely protective of.

'Look, they were a nightmare to come off. I promised myself to ride it out if the anxiety ever came back.' I had never made that promise to myself, but for some mysterious reason, my heels were digging into a hill I didn't know I was standing on. I wanted to leave. This felt like an ambush.

'Right, well, there are other antidepressants. Better ones for antenatal mental health care as well.' She was looking at me hopefully. Her tone was calm but she was twisting her wedding ring a lot. Was she nervous? Was she nervous of me?

'I don't want it. I'm fine. Please stop asking me if I'm okay. I have to go.' I stood up.

She almost winded me when she turned back to her computer and said, 'Okay, noted. I will need to see Ari again tomorrow, though. I have to measure his head.'

Again?! Was she mental? How much could it grow in twenty-four hours?

'Fine,' I said. 'Of course you do.' I stormed to the reception to be ignored by the three women until one informed me I'd been bulk-billed again. Well, at least this shitshow wasn't expensive.

I returned home to bitch about the incompetent GP and questioned why on earth Ari needed daily visits when he seemed perfectly fine now. Surely this was overkill! Mum and Lukasz listened patiently and convinced me that she must know what she was doing.

The next day I begrudgingly showed up to the GP, ready to tell her to stick it up her jumper. She measured Ari's head, and jotted it down on a piece of paper. She seemed nervous, probably because I looked as sour as a human can look.

'Well,' she said. 'His head is the same as it was yesterday, so that's good. But there is one other thing I want to talk to you about, Bron. I've called a few mental health professionals and got their specialised opinion on medicine that might help you.'

Oh. My. God. I could have screamed. Is this about me again?

'And I know you didn't have a good experience getting off them last time,' she continued, 'but there is one that's quick onset and quick offset. This could make all this much easier and much more enjoyable for you.' She scanned my face for a reaction, but I had none.

The penny dropped. What exactly was I pushing back on? This woman was offering me a pill that might make this hellscape tolerable. I suddenly remembered how much easier my life was when I took antidepressants last time, and as I looked down at Ari, it dawned on me that I could actually be enjoying this time with him if I let her help me. I sheepishly surrendered and she handed me a script she'd printed out before I had even arrived.

I went straight to the chemist and swallowed one of the tablets in the car without water. I didn't realise how desperate I'd been to escape the darkness, and it's likely I prolonged it because I felt like that's where I needed to be. I felt sheepish that I had fought this GP tooth and nail, and also that I didn't see that all these appointments were actually for me.

She played that perfectly. If she'd asked me to come in for me, I would never have returned. In fact, if she'd overtly told me that I was not okay and that my health was her biggest concern, I probably would have seen Dr Creep before I saw her again.

Within a day of taking the medicine the muscles in my face had re-engaged and the colour in my life started to bleed back in. I don't even think it kicks in that quickly, but the placebo effect was enough for me to feel lighter. That first pill took the weight off my shoulders and I felt like I could do what I had set out to do: not only to be a good mum to my kids but to actually enjoy it. Success!

I had hated almost every GP I ever saw. I'd had enough negative experiences with some of them to not trust any of them – from prescribing me the contraceptive pill without any warning of the hormonal hellscape that accompanied it, to making me feel shame for being a woman in the first place. This GP, however, saved my life and gave me the medicine to be the mum I desperately wanted to be.

I emailed her the next day thanking her for the medicine and said she was right all along. Her response wasn't emotional (I would have hated that), just a simple *My pleasure. Take care of yourself.* The concept of taking care of a mother so she could take care of herself was not something I grew up witnessing. Mother's Day is much bigger than Father's Day because it's easy to buy things that mothers usually neglect to buy themselves – slippers, massages, candles. Society tells mothers to put themselves last, so it's actually a Christmas fucking miracle when any mother is perfectly fine.

The GP stopped asking me to come in to measure Ari's head after that, because she never had to measure it in the first place. It goes without saying that I am a wildly annoying patient. I'm stubborn, pigheaded and impatient and, while most GPs would have loved to never have me in their office even once, this GP kept dragging me back in over and over until I let her fix me. If she ever reads this book, I want her to know I owe her the life I lead today (and probably an apology as well, lol).

The day after I started taking the medicine I was holding Ari and making myself a cup of tea, and Lukasz asked if I was okay, a question I had grown accustomed to. Instead of my catchphrase, 'Stop asking me if I'm okay', I said, 'Actually, I think I'm going to be.'

EPILOGUE

So there you have it: my book.

I'm writing this in my bedroom as the Melbourne winter sun streams through my window. My desk is strewn with children's drawings, empty tea cups, stray buttons and a parking fine I can't bring myself to pay (damn you to hell, Merri-Bek Council). I have remnants of last night's makeup on from a gig I did last night, where I was crowned 'Miss Belconnen' (long story), and my jeans are bursting at the seams from stress eating to meet this deadline.

The book is due today.

Eighteen months ago, my manager, Bec (a powerhouse of a woman who has changed countless people's lives, including mine), called me and said, 'I think you have a book in you.' I laughed nervously because I was certain I did not have time to write a bloody book, but I also knew she was right. In fact, I definitely didn't have the time, but I wouldn't dare disappoint that goddess, so I agreed. I missed deadline after deadline, not because I was writing so much, but because I wasn't writing at all. I was terrified of what would happen if I put my most vulnerable experiences on paper and forced myself to literally sit face to face with them. I cried more times writing this book than I care to admit. Some of the chapters hit nerves I thought I had buried for good; other chapters I approached thinking they were going to be pure comedy gold, only to end up tapping into a vein so packed with trauma that I found myself drowning all over again.

It is no secret that I have an avoidant attachment style. It's apparently not very trendy, but I am fond of it, so sorry/not sorry. As much as I love it, it did make this book excruciating to write at times; but I promised myself one thing, and that was to be as honest as possible – I owed that to each version of my past self. From the teenage girl who lost her mum for years to a menopausal snap, to the young mum who found herself fighting The Noise with mental and physical punishment, through to the mum sitting in a black hole with the baby boy she'd almost lost. My heart bleeds for those versions of me, and I would be lying if I said I wasn't scared of what my brain is capable of next.

I hope that next time I go mad (and trust me, I know I will), I am kinder to myself, that I let Lukasz in faster, and that I remember that my mistakes don't define me. Because our mistakes don't define us – our ability to move on does.

Thanks to the Coolamon swimming pool, I still hate learning but, even so, I've unintentionally learnt a lot since becoming a mother. Perhaps the most important lesson of all is that, as hard as motherhood is, I would never have it any other way.

And to the mum at the park I let down with my silence, I hope this book reaches you and you know that I will forever be in awe of your fight to survive the hot flames of hell that motherhood can dish up. I raise my glass to you, and any other mother out there who has fought the good fight and won.

ACKNOWLEDGEMENTS

This book did not come out of nowhere and, while it will be my name on the front cover, I am not the only one responsible for it. Thank you to the following people:

My manager, Bec, for pushing me to write this. I have practised hours of speeches to you about how I bit off more than I could chew and I would like to return the cash advance to the publisher. Thank you for being formidable enough that I could never actually pull the pin. You're worth your weight in gold, and I would say that even if you were the size of a house.

My sounding boards, Claire, Laurence and Hamish, for reading some of my scribblings. Thanks for knowing me well enough to know what I was trying to say, and encouraging me to lean in when all I wanted to do was throw my laptop in the Yarra. I would love to say I would do the same for you, but I'm too busy – blame Bec.

Hels, my mum. You were gracious enough to allow me to share your darkest days, and I am certain your generosity will help some people feel less alone. Menopause is a mysterious beast, and you may have scars, but you conquered it triumphantly. Ever since the age of four, you have been a strong, axe-wielding woman, and I feel honoured to have watched you rise like a phoenix after having half of your head chopped off. No mother is perfect, and you are no exception, but you are my mum and I love you endlessly. Now, put your ciggie out and go write your own book. It's going to be phenomenal.

Lukasz, you have been, as always (except for Ari's labour *never forget*), incredibly and unwaveringly supportive. I don't know if many people who would be totally comfortable with their partner writing a memoir but, unlike me, you believe in everything I do. I hope you don't mind, but I am sharing the message you sent me this morning:

> *I just read the chapter 'Black and White Tiles' and it's beautiful. Like when you're on stage and I can't look away, I couldn't stop reading it. I'm so glad you found your thing, babe. I'm going to do everything in my power to help you be the best. I think the world needs you.*

Lukasz, I hope you feel the same way after reading the other chapters. I don't have high hopes you'll love the chapter about Ari's labour, but that's absolutely your fault. Sorry for throwing so many curveballs at you – you've met roughly forty different versions of me, and I am unbelievably lucky that you've found love for all of them, even when I have not liked them even a little bit. Never once, in all my moments of self-loathing, did I ever feel unloved by you, which is truly mind-blowing. I don't know what I did to deserve you.

My children. My beautiful, perfectly imperfect children. Olive, Edie and Ari, I am eternally proud of you. As hard as motherhood kicked me, you were the prize worth fighting for. You always, always will be. I want to apologise for slipping when you were babies and I hope you have absolutely no memories of it. You weren't the cause, either – you were the reasons to keep going. I also want to apologise in advance for when I lose my mind again, because I will. Menopause will change me and test my very fibres, but I will always come back to you. This I promise.